Changi

TWO

Changing Higher Education seeks to make sense of the many changes that have taken place in learning and teaching in higher education and to offer insights into how learning and teaching in higher education might develop in the future.

Building on the important work of Lewis Elton, leading researchers and practitioners in the field examine and reflect on different aspects of these changes. Focusing on five key areas, they:

- Outline changes in higher education and ways of thinking about learning and teaching in higher education that have occurred over the last 30 years.
- Analyse the development of students' learning in higher education.
- Examine the development of learning technologies in higher education.
- Consider the development of the accreditation and scholarship of teaching in higher education.
- Develop a framework through which to understand and question the future development of learning and teaching in higher education.

Changing Higher Education provides an in-depth analysis of the changes in learning and teaching that have taken place over the last 30 years. It offers staff and educational developers, and those studying postgraduate qualifications in learning and teaching in higher education, an insightful framework through which to understand and question current and future developments in learning and teaching in higher education.

Paul Ashwin is a lecturer in post-compulsory education in the Department of Educational Research, Lancaster University. His research interests are focused on learning and teaching in higher education and within this context include phenomenography, students' approaches to learning, and critical pedagogy. Prior to joining Lancaster University, he spent four years researching students' experiences of learning at the Institute for the Advancement of Learning, University of Oxford.

The staff and educational development series
Series editor: Professor James Wisdom

A Guide to Staff and Educational Development
Edited by Peter Kahn and David Baume

Inspiring Students
Edited by Stephen Fallows and Kemal Abmet

The Management of Independent Learning
Edited by Jo Tait and Peter Knight

Managing Educational Development Projects
Effective management for maximum impact
Edited by Carole Baume, Paul Martin and Mantz Yorke

Motivating Students
Edited by Sally Brown, Steve Armstrong and Gail Thompson

Research, Teaching and Learning in Higher Education
Edited by Peter Knight

Reshaping Teaching in Higher Education
Linking teaching with research
Edited by Alan Jenkins, Rosanna Breen and Roger Lindsay

Resource-Based Learning
Edited by Sally Brown and Brenda Smith

Teaching International Students
Edited by Jude Carroll and Jeanette Ryan

SEDA is the Staff and Educational Development Association. It supports and encourages developments in teaching and learning in higher education through a variety of methods: publications, conferences, networking, journals, regional meetings and research – and through various SEDA Accreditations Schemes.

SEDA
Selly Wick House
59–61 Selly Wick Road
Selly Park
Birmingham B29 7JE
Tel: 0121 415 6801
Fax: 0121 415 6802
Email: office@seda.ac.uk
Website: www.seda.ac.uk

Changing Higher Education

The development of learning and teaching

Edited by Paul Ashwin

Routledge
Taylor & Francis Group

LONDON AND NEW YORK

First published 2006 by Routledge
2 Park Square, Milton Park, Abingdon, Oxon, OX14 4RN

Simultaneously published in the USA and Canada
by Taylor & Francis Inc
270 Madison Avenue, New York, NY 10016

Routledge is an imprint of the Taylor & Francis Group

© 2006 Paul Ashwin and contributors

Typeset in Gill Sans by GreenGate Publishing Services, Tonbridge
Printed and bound in Great Britain by TJ International Ltd, Padstow,
Cornwall

British Library Cataloguing in Publication Data
A catalogue record for this book is available from the British Library

Library of Congress Cataloging in Publication Data
Changing higher education : the development of learning and teaching /
edited by Paul Ashwin.– 1st.
       p. cm. – (Staff and Educational Development Association series)
Includes bibliographical references and index.
1. College teaching–Great Britain. 2. Adult learning–Great Britain.
3. Education, Higher–Great Britain. 4. Educational technology–Great
Britain. 5. Educational change–Great Britain. I. Ashwin, Paul, 1970- II. Series:
SEDA series

LB2331.C4545 2005
378.2'1–dc22

                                                                    2005005685

ISBN 0-415-34128-0 (hbk)
ISBN 0-415-34129-9 (pbk)

For Lewis

Contents

Foreword

It is fitting that Lewis Elton should be honoured by a book titled *Changing Higher Education: The Development of Learning and Teaching*.

When Lewis began his work it was generally assumed that all that was required to teach in higher education was a graduate degree in one's discipline. Knowledge of the subject matter was all that mattered. Lewis was one of the first to recognise that the professor's knowledge counted for little if students were not learning. Effective teaching depends not only on the teacher's knowledge but also upon the teacher's skills and strategies for teaching. These skills, like skills in other fields, need to be taught and learned and practised.

Lewis is a pioneer in training university teachers. His work extends beyond the United Kingdom to the Far East and worldwide. His personal contributions are augmented and extended by the outstanding students he trained – many of whom are represented by chapters in this volume.

I am honoured to pay tribute to one of the towering figures in the field I love – teaching and learning in higher education!

Wilbert. J. McKeachie
Professor Emeritus
University of Michigan

Preface

The purpose of this book is to chart the development of teaching and learning in higher education, from the perspective of the students and colleagues of one of the greatest figures in this area – Lewis Elton. As such it both honours Lewis's work, and emphasises its continuing relevance to the changing world of university learning and teaching.

The way in which this book acts as a tribute to Lewis Elton's work is to provide some original insights into the developments that have taken place in learning and teaching in higher education over the last 30 years. Most of the authors explicitly draw on Lewis's work but, more than this, we all draw on the spirit in which Lewis conducts his work and the deep interest and commitment that he has demonstrated toward so many aspects of learning and teaching in higher education. His writing in this area has covered a diverse range of topics including change in higher education, educational technology, the accreditation of teaching, assessment, doctoral supervision, academic development, the relations between teaching and research, distance learning, student learning and motivation, and educational leadership. And, with an average of nearly three publications a year over 40 years, this list is by no means comprehensive. Beyond his writing, we, as well as others across the globe, have benefited from Lewis's wisdom and generosity as a teacher. We are delighted to have this opportunity to recognise the work of one of the world leaders and pioneers in the field of learning and teaching in higher education.

The editor and contributors

Notes on the editor and contributors

Paul Ashwin is a lecturer in the Department of Educational Research, Lancaster University. His PhD focused on peer learning, during which he was fortunate enough to benefit from the outstanding supervision of Lewis Elton. Paul has published widely in this area, as well as on teaching and learning in higher education. This work includes research into students' and teachers' conceptions of tutorials, which was completed whilst he was Research Fellow at the Institute for the Advancement of University Learning, University of Oxford.

Liz Beaty is Director (Learning and Teaching) at the Higher Education Funding Council for England. She is responsible for northern regions and for learning and teaching policy including the Centres for Excellence in Teaching and Learning (CETLs) and relationships with the Quality Assurance Agency and the Higher Education Academy. Liz gained her PhD from Surrey University and her research and practice has built upon the foundation provided by Lewis Elton at that time, and this has been kept alive through useful discussions ever since. Her career has included educational research at the Open University and educational and management development at Northumbria, Brighton and more recently Coventry University where she was Director of the Centre for Higher Education Development. She ran the teacher accreditation scheme for the UK Staff and Educational Development Association (SEDA), and was co-chair of SEDA from 1996 to 2000. Her publications span students' experiences of higher education, experiential and action learning, and strategies for educational change.

David Boud is Professor of Adult Education in the Faculty of Education at the University of Technology, Sydney. He was Lewis Elton's first full-time research student in education when he established the Institute for Educational Technology at the University of Surrey in 1969. He has been involved in research and development in adult, higher and professional education since that time and has contributed extensively to the literature, including 14 books written or edited with various others. His most recent are *Peer Learning in Higher Education* (Kogan Page, 2001) with Ruth Cohen and Jane Sampson, and *Work-Based Learning: A New Higher Education*

(Open University Press, 2001) with Nicky Solomon. *Productive Reflection and Learning at Work* with Peter Cressey and Peter Docherty (RoutledgeFalmer) should appear in 2005.

Will Bridge is Head of the London College of Communication – the largest constituent college of the University of the Arts London. Since completing one of the UK's first PhD studies in the field of educational technology with Lewis Elton, who was pioneering this field at Surrey University, he has worked in industry, further and higher education, and in the higher education policy branch of government. His initial interest in non-traditional higher education teaching and evaluation methods has developed over recent years into the expansion and requirements of non-traditional learners in higher education, the interface between further and higher education, and the development of vocational degree and sub-degree programmes.

Pam Denicolo, Professor of Postgraduate and Professional Education, is the director of the Graduate School for the Social Sciences and of the Centre for Inter-Professional and Postgraduate Education and Training for the School of Pharmacy at the University of Reading. She has published widely on personal construct psychology, academic staff development and professional education. She is the secretary/treasurer of the International Study Association on Teachers and Teaching (ISATT) and an Honorary Member of the Royal Pharmaceutical Society of Great Britain (RPSGB). Her current research interests include: an exploration of doctoral training and assessment, different understandings and implementations of the process; the development of more effective teaching and learning at senior levels in the Health and Social Services; and more effective communication within and between different professional participants in teams concerned with healthcare. Her current activities owe much to her formative years in higher education during the 1980s when she was first a doctoral student in the team led by Lewis Elton and then accompanied him around the world running Academic Staff Development workshops.

Vivien Hodgson is Professor of Networked Management Learning in the Department of Management Learning at Lancaster University Management School and director of the Centre for Studies in Advanced Learning Technology (CSALT). She has carried out research on students' experiences of learning in higher education since the mid 1970s and on the use of technology to support open learning since 1988. Her interest in learning and the learner's experience began in 1975, when she was offered a doctoral studentship at Surrey University to undertake a study of the lecture method in science education under the supervision of Lewis Elton. His help and support at that time, and since, led to a lifelong interest in learning and researching the learner's experience. She has written extensively on the issues related to the introduction and the learner's experience of networked learning in higher and management education. Her many publications in the field include *Beyond Distance Teaching: Towards Open Learning* (Open University Press, 1987). She is coordinator of the E-quality in E-learning (EQUEL) European centre of excellence and European editor for the *Journal of Computer Assisted Learning*.

Diana Laurillard is Head of the e-Learning Strategy Unit at the Department for Education and Skills, where she has been responsible for the government's strategy Harnessing Technology: Transforming Learning and Children's Services. She was previously Professor of Educational Technology and Pro-Vice-Chancellor for Learning Technologies and Teaching at The Open University. She has spent over 25 years in research, development and evaluation of interactive mutimedia materials and internet services in education and training, covering a wide range of discipline areas. She has made a significant contribution to fundamental research on the relationship between student learning and learning technologies, recognized in her honorary degrees and awards. She is a Fellow of the Royal Society of Arts, a Visiting Professor at the Institute of Education, and an Honorary Fellow of University College London. Her book *Rethinking University Teaching* (Routledge Falmer, Second Edition, 2002) has been widely acclaimed, and is used as a set book in courses on learning technology all over the world. In 1974 Lewis Elton enabled her to make the radical change from Lecturer in Mathematics tat the Polytechnic of the South Bank to a research post in the then neascent field of Computer Assisted Learning at the University of Surrey, where he also supervised her part-time PhD on student learning.

David McConnell is a researcher and practitioner of networked online learning and teaching. He has been involved in the field since the 1970s when he took his PhD at Surrey University under the supervision of Lewis Elton, who helped him come to a fuller understanding of the nature of learning and teaching in higher education settings. David has pioneered many innovations in higher education learning and teaching and was one of the first people in the UK to develop computer mediated communications in distance learning in the early 1980s while at the UK Open University. He co-pioneered the first UK online Masters in Management Learning at Lancaster University. David is currently Professor of Higher Education in the department of Educational Research, Lancaster University, and was previously Professor in the School of Education at the University of Sheffield, where he was Director of the Masters in Networked E-Learning, an innovative global course which he designed in 1996 and on which he has been teaching ever since. He has published extensively in academic journals and has written several books. His book *Implementing Computer Supported Collaborative Learning* (Kogan Page, 1994 and 2000) is a key text on distance learning Masters' courses across the globe. He founded the Networked Learning Conference in 1998. His research interests are in continuing professional development, cultural and pedagogic issues in online learning (especially groups and communities), and collaborative online assessment.

Lorraine Stefani is currently Professor and Director of the Centre for Professional Development at the University of Auckland. Prior to this she was a Reader in Academic Practice at the University of Strathclyde in Glasgow, Scotland. She has influenced the academic development agenda in UK higher education through being an active member of the ILTHE Council, the governing body of the Institute for Learning and Teaching in Higher Education; through her strong links with the Quality Assurance Agency for Higher Education (Scotland); and through her role as Chair of the Personal Development Planning in Higher Education (Scotland) Network. She is known for her work on the assessment of student learning, accreditation of academic practice, the scholarship of teaching and learning and the implementation of professional development planning strategies. In 1997, she completed a postgraduate diploma in Higher Education Research and Development at University College London under the tutorship of Lewis Elton.

Introduction

Chapter 1

The development of learning and teaching in higher education

The changing context

Paul Ashwin

This book is about the development of learning and teaching in higher education. In particular, it examines developments in learning, learning technologies and teaching in higher education that have occurred over approximately the last 30 years. It examines these developments in a number of ways and from a number of perspectives. Different chapters look at different aspects of learning and teaching and do so in different ways. However, there are two things that hold these chapters together. First, there is a commitment to start with the learner, be they student or teacher, when thinking about ways of developing learning and teaching in higher education. Second, there is a commitment to making sense of past changes in learning and teaching in higher education in order to offer an insight into how they might be developed in the future.

The developments in learning, learning technologies and teaching in higher education that are considered in this book did not take place in a vacuum. They have, to some extent, been driven by changes in higher education more generally, by changes in government policy relating to learning and teaching in higher education, and by changes in the way learning and teaching in higher education have been conceptualised and researched. For this reason, the purpose of this chapter is to set the context for the rest of the book by briefly examining each of these areas in turn. I will then outline the other chapters in this book and so give an overview of changes in a number of aspects of learning and teaching in higher education.

Changes in British higher education

It is commonplace to talk about the high level of change in higher education over about the last 30 years (for example see Scott 1995, Becher and Trowler 2001). These changes have undoubtedly had a huge impact on the development of learning and teaching in higher education.

In this chapter, I will focus on changes in the British higher education system between 1972–3 and 2002–3, with a particular focus on the English system. The reason for focusing on the British higher education system is to give an in-depth analysis of the context of changes in learning and teaching within a single system of higher education, although similar changes have taken place in many countries

(Scott 1995). The reason for focusing on this 30-year period is that 1972–3 was the first year in which all of the polytechnics formed after the Robbins Report (Committee on Higher Education 1963) had been formally recognised by the Secretary of State for Education. As such, a comparison across this timeframe is a comparison across a broadly similar sized higher education system.

Rather than give an historical account of the development of change in higher education, I will examine the differences between the British higher education system in the years 1973 and 2003 and thus set the context for changes in learning and teaching in higher education. In doing so, I will examine a number of interrelated areas of change in higher education: changes in the higher education system, changes in government spending on higher education, changes in what the government sees as the purpose of higher education, changes in student numbers, changes in student diversity, and institutional changes in higher education.

Changes in the higher education system

The British higher education system in 1973 was very different from the system in 2003. In fact it was not a single system. Rather, there was a binary divide between universities (now referred to as 'old universities') and polytechnics (now referred to as 'new universities'), with the universities funded centrally through the Universities Grants Committee (UGC) and the polytechnics funded locally through the Local Education Authorities (LEAs). The different types of institutions were intended to provide different types of higher education, with the universities focused on a 'traditional' research-led education and the polytechnics being vocationally orientated. The binary divide between universities and polytechnics was ended in 1992, with all of the former polytechnics eventually adopting the title of 'university', and both are now funded through separate funding councils for England, Wales and Scotland, and through the Department for Employment and Learning in Northern Ireland. Many policy decisions regarding higher education in Scotland and Wales have also been devolved to the Scottish Parliament and the Welsh Assembly respectively.

The 30 polytechnics had been established in response to the 1963 Robbins Report (DES 1975), which had also seen the number of universities increase from 23 to 45 (Williams 1977). Thus, this was a time of expansion in higher education, which was to come to an abrupt end as a result of the spending cuts of 1973. However, the system has since expanded further with the current number of universities having increased by about 50 per cent on the number of old universities and polytechnics in 1972–3. These additional universities have come largely from the colleges of higher education, which underwent similar changes to the polytechnics in the ways that they were funded. In addition, higher education is increasingly being delivered in Further Education colleges, especially the new two-year foundation degrees, which involve business in offering a vocationally focused education.

Thus we have seen an expansion in the higher education system and an apparent levelling out, as the new universities have increasingly begun to emulate the old universities by combining research and teaching. However, as we shall see in later sections, there are many ways in which the higher education system remains firmly divided.

Changes in government spending

As the number of universities has increased, there has been an associated increase in government funding. Between 1976 and 1995, there was a real-terms increase of 45 per cent in government spending on higher education (National Committee of Inquiry into Higher Education (NCIHE) 1997a, paragraph 3.93). However, it is important to recognise that this represents a fall in the proportion of the nation's resources that are committed to higher education, with the proportion of the UK's Gross Domestic Product (GDP) that is spent on higher education falling from 1.2 per cent in 1976 (NCIHE 1997a, paragraph 3.94) to 0.8 per cent in 2003 (DfES 2003a).

Changes in the government's aims for higher education

As the amount that the government spends on higher education has increased, so the government's aims for higher education appear to have shifted. Whilst the role of higher education in developing the nation's economy was made clear in the Robbins Report (Committee on Higher Education 1963), this aim seemed to have a similar weight to the other aims of developing the intellect of the person, developing knowledge, and developing society. However, the recent English Higher Education White Paper (DfES 2003a) appeared to emphasise that it was the vocational nature of higher education that was most valued:

> In a fast-changing and increasingly competitive world, the role of higher education in equipping the labour force with appropriate and relevant skills, in stimulating innovation and supporting productivity and in enriching the quality of life is central.
>
> (DfES 2003a, paragraph 1.3: 10)

Changes in student numbers

Whilst the number of universities increased, the real expansion was in the number of students studying in higher education over this period. For example, the number of full-time students in higher education increased nearly four times from about 343,000 in 1973 (Williams 1977) to 1.3 million in 2003 (HESA 2004). The age participation index (the proportion of 18–20 year olds engaging in higher education) has increased from 14 per cent in 1973 (Williams 1973) to 35 per cent in 2003 (HESA 2004), which in Trow's (1973) terms represents a shift from an 'elite' to a 'mass' higher education system and close to a 'universal' system of higher education.

Despite the increase in funding for higher education indicated above, the funding per student fell by 40 per cent between 1976 and 1995 (NCIHE 1997a, paragraph 3.95). Student–teacher ratios have also increased from about 1 teacher to 8 students in universities, and 1 teacher to 6 students in the polytechnics, in 1973 (calculated from UGC 1975 and DES 1975)[1] to 1 teacher to 18 students in 2003 (HESA 2004).

Thus, whilst the number of students in higher education has expanded rapidly, the resources available for learning and teaching have fallen considerably over this period, both in terms of the sizes of student groups and in the resources available to support learning and teaching.

Changes in student diversity

In terms of increases in diversity of the student body, there have been some marked changes with regard to gender and race. However, the changes in terms of diversity of social class and disability have been less marked.

There has been a huge increase in the proportion of female students studying in higher education. In 1972–3, only 29 per cent of full-time students studying in higher education were women (calculated from Williams 1977). In 2002–3, 55 per cent of full-time undergraduates were women (HESA 2004).

In terms of race, the increase is more difficult to substantiate, as figures were not collected on the levels of ethnic minorities in higher education (itself an indication of how times have changed). However, a small-scale study as part of the Rampton Report (Committee of Inquiry into the Education of Children from Ethnic Minority Groups 1981), which looked at higher education participation amongst Asian and West Indian students in six inner city Local Education Authorities, found that about 1 per cent of eighteen-year-olds of 'West Indian' origin and 3 per cent of eighteen-year-olds of 'Asian' origin went on to higher education compared with 11 per cent of the whole population. In comparison, based on 2001 figures, Gilchrist et al. (2003) argued that students from ethnic minorities were 'over represented' in higher education, making up 14.6 per cent of the higher education population compared to 8.5 per cent of the general population of 15- to 21-year-olds. However, the picture is mixed with some groups, such as young people from a Pakistani and Bangladeshi background, being underrepresented. Equally, there is evidence that students from ethnic minorities are not gaining access to the more presitigious 'old' universities. For example, Hogarth et al. (1997) reported that 73 per cent of black students were studying at 'new' universities (the old polytechnics).

In terms of social class, the increase in student numbers has not been uniform across different classes. In fact the gap between the proportion of those participating in higher education from socio-economic groups I, II and IIIn and those participating from groups IIIm, IV and V has grown from 27 per cent in 1970 (NCIHE 1997b, Table 1.1) to 31 per cent in 2001 (DfES 2003a). In other words, whilst participation in higher education has increased in all socio-economic groups, it has risen fastest amongst those from 'higher' socio-economic groups. These groups are significantly over-represented in higher education. Again there is also a difference between the prestige of the institutions that students from different classes gain access to. Ashworth (2004) found that there was a very high negative correlation between the research quality of an institution (as measured by the Research Assessment Exercise (RAE)) and low parental class of –0.89. Equally, there was a high negative correlation between the level of teaching quality of institutions and low parental class of –0.65. Thus, not only has the relative participation of students from lower socio-economic groups not kept pace with students from higher socio-economic groups, the institutions to which they have access are less prestigious.

With regard to the diversity of students in terms of age, there is a mixed picture of change. In 1972–3, 21 per cent of all students were over 21 (Woodley 1981), compared to 60 per cent of students in 2002–3 (HESA 2004). This shows a massive increase in the number and proportion of mature students. However, this increase has largely been in part-time study. Woodley (1981) reported that in 1976, 8 per cent of full-time undergraduates were over 25; in 2002–3 this figure had risen slightly to 11 per cent.

The proportion of disabled students has increased. Sturt (1981) reported that in 1972–3, there were 554 disabled students in higher education making up about 0.2 per cent of the population (as opposed to 0.9 per cent of the general population). In 2003, students with disabilities made up 6 per cent of the higher education population (HESA 2004), compared to 15 per cent of the working age population (Riddell et al. 2002). Whilst the level of under-representation is difficult to quantify, as some disabled people would not qualify for higher education, it seems likely that disabled people are still excluded from higher education due to a mixture of financial, physical and cultural barriers (Riddell et al. 2002).

So, whilst there have been some positive changes in the diversity of students in higher education, there are still appear to be some barriers in terms of access to those from working-class backgrounds and those with disabilities, as well as to some groups of students gaining access to the more prestigious institutions.

Institutional changes

As the number and diversity of students has increased, the structures of courses have changed. Trowler (1998) shows how there has been a shift in the credit framework in British higher education, from a system where students largely studied one or two disciplines to one where students can put together their own degrees from a number of different modules. These changes have taken place at a different pace in different institutions, with some institutions, most notably the Open University which had a modular curriculum from its inception in the late 1960s, leading the way on modularisation and other universities still not being modularised. Trowler (1998) reports that by 1996 about 80 per cent of universities were modularised or partly modularised.

The impact of changes in British higher education on the development of learning and teaching

The effects of these changes in higher education on the experience of learning and teaching have been huge. Tutors and students tend to be learning and teaching in larger, more diverse groups on modules that draw students from a number of degree courses rather than from single courses. These modules are less well funded than the courses were in the past. These changes have led to an increased focus in government policy on learning and teaching in higher education and a change in the way that learning and teaching in higher education has been conceptualised and researched. The next two sections of this chapter will focus on each of these issues in turn.

Government policy and learning and teaching in higher education

Compared to the early 1970s the amount of government interest in learning and teaching in higher education in the UK is immense. As government spending on higher education has grown, there has been an increase in the amount of regulation of learning and teaching in order to ensure that taxpayers are getting value for money. This regulation has only increased as students and their families, especially in England, have been expected to meet some of the costs of higher education. . Employers of these new graduates have increasingly called for universities to ensure that they are producing graduates who are ready for the job market. In response to these pressures, there has been a two-pronged strategy. On the one hand, the level of central regulation of learning and teaching has increased, whilst on the other, a number of recent policy initiatives have encouraged universities to change by offering financial incentives for the development of learning and teaching.

In the early 1970s, there were different systems in place for the regulation of learning and teaching in the universities and polytechnics. The universities were largely self-regulating through their senates and the system of external examiners, whilst polytechnics had their standards set by the CNAA (Council for National Academic Awards) and the quality of learning and teaching was inspected by the HMI (Her Majesty's Inspectorate for Education). When the binary divide was removed in 1992, the polytechnic model was introduced across the system (Elton and Cryer 1994, Evans and Abbot 1998) and since 1997 this work has been carried out by the QAA (Quality Assurance Agency in Higher Education). This increased regulation of learning and teaching is likely to continue as European countries attempt to make their undergraduate and postgraduate degrees comparable as part of the Bologna process. This is intended to establish a European area of higher education by 2010, in order to allow students, teachers and researchers freedom of movement across higher education in Europe.

As well as increased regulation, there has been a massive increase in the amount of central support available for the development of learning and teaching.

Gibbs *et al.* (2000) report that up until 1980 the development of teaching was seen as the responsibility for individual lecturers rather than the focus of departmental, institutional or government policy. The situation has altered radically since then. For example, in England, HEFCE (Higher Education Funding Council for England) allocated about £30 million a year from 1999 to 2005 to support the quality of learning and teaching through the Teaching Quality Enhancement Fund (TQEF) (see HEFCE 2005 for further information). This fund seeks to support learning and teaching at a number of different levels. At the level of the individual teacher, the quality of learning and teaching is supported through the annual award of 50 (increased from 20 since 2004) National Teaching Fellowship Awards (NTFS), which reward individual academics who demonstrate excellence in learning and teaching. At the institutional level, institutions have been entitled to money to support learning and teaching provided they develop a satisfactory institutional learning and teaching strategy. Unusually, individual institutions have had autonomy in deciding which aspects of learning and teaching they will spend this money on. At the subject level, the Learning and Teaching Support Network (LTSN) was introduced, which involves 24 subject centres that seek to provide disciplinary based learning and teaching support. This work will be further added to by the development of Centres for Excellence in Teaching and Learning (CETL). Some £315 million is available to fund CETLs over the five-year period from 2004–5 to 2008–9. The purpose of CETLs is to reward excellent teaching practice and to invest in that practice further in order to increase and deepen its impact across a wider learning and teaching community. Finally, there is the Higher Education Academy (HEA), previously the Institute for Learning and Teaching in Higher Education (ILTHE)), which includes some aspects of the TQEF (for example the LTSN) and with which individual practitioners can become registered to demonstrate their expertise in learning and teaching. The HEA is currently working towards developing professional standards for academic practice and continuing professional development in higher education.

Whilst it is clear that there is more central regulation and support for the development of learning and teaching, there are a number of potential problems with this strategy. First, the administrative load of the regulatory system has reduced the time that academics have available to spend thinking and developing their teaching (Trowler 2003). Second, in terms of the support available, it is not clear what model of change is underpinning these policies or, in other words, how these different initiatives are intended to develop learning and teaching in a sustainable way. For example, it is not clear how giving 50 academics a year £50,000 each to further develop their already excellent teaching will lead to an improvement in teaching across the higher education sector. Equally, much of the support available is short term, with institutions expected to take over the funding of the institutional aspects of TQEF. Finally, and most significantly, the amount that is available to support learning and teaching is dwarfed by that available for excellent research (more than £8 billion available over six years in the 2008 Research Assessment Exercise (RAE)). This has led many academics to focus on their

rather than their teaching, with teaching increasingly being left to teach-
stants and temporary staff (Elton 2000).

has left learning and teaching in higher education in a somewhat ambiguous position. At one level it is more regulated than it was 30 years ago and there is
more central support for the development of learning and teaching than ever
before. On the other hand, much of this support is short term and is small compared to the amount available for excellent research. However, despite its
problems, this additional support has been useful in developing learning and
teaching in response to the changes in higher education that were described in the
previous section.

Changes in thinking and research into learning and teaching in higher education

As well as changes in the central regulation and support of learning and teaching
in higher education, the thinking and research that underpins learning and teaching in higher education has changed significantly over the last 30 years. In order
to show this, I will compare the concerns expressed in books written about learning and teaching in the early 1970s with those published more recently. In
undertaking such a comparison, three differences are immediately apparent. First,
there is a difference in what is focused on in learning and teaching; second, there
is a difference in the research that is drawn upon when thinking about learning
and teaching; and third, different types of theory are used to underpin this
research into learning and teaching in higher education.

The focus in books on learning and teaching written in the early 1970s is on
teaching methods. In Beard's (1970) book the focus is on what forms of teaching
methods are appropriate to meet different kinds of educational objectives. There
are chapters focused on the lecture method, teaching in small groups, and practical and laboratory teaching. There are also chapters on instruction without a
teacher and independent study, where the focus is on the work students do outside
of the lecture theatre or seminar room. Equally, Bligh's (1971) book is focused on
what lectures are appropriate for, and MacKenzie *et al.* (1970) focus on different
teaching methods and media for teaching. The focus, then, appeared to be on
finding out which teaching methods were most appropriate for supporting students in learning particular aspects of their disciplines. For example, as Beard
(1968) proposed:

> What is needed is a concerted effort in studying each method, collecting
> information already available and experimenting with variety in method to
> see which ones are effective and under what circumstances.
>
> (Beard 1968: 54)

This meant that the focus was on what the teacher did and how they organised the
curriculum for students. In more recent books on learning and teaching, there is a

marked shift to think about how students experience their learning environment. Ramsden (2003) spends as many chapters examining students' learning as he does examining ways of teaching. When teaching is considered, it is not divided by different methods of teaching but rather into different aspects of the learning and teaching experience: course design, teaching strategies and assessment. Biggs (1999) has a similar focus that is reflected in his title *Teaching for Quality Learning at University: What the Student Does*. There is equally recognition that different teachers might use the same teaching method differently and that what is key is what teachers focus on in their teaching (the subject matter, the students, or their learning) rather than simply the particular methods they use.

It is argued then that there has been a shift in focus over time onto students' experiences of learning, and using a consideration of these experiences as a way of thinking about how to organise teaching. This change is in part due to the explosion in research into learning and teaching in higher education over the past 30 years or so. For example, Beard (1968) reported that between 1960 and 1968, there were 144 studies of teaching methods in higher education in the UK. Tight (2003) reports that in the year 2000 there were 164 articles on learning and teaching, course design or the student experience published in 17 English language education journals outside of North America. Whilst there is great difficulty in making such a comparison, this represents a nine-fold increase in the number of papers published on learning and teaching. With this increase in research into learning and teaching in higher education has come a focus on the student learning experience, driven mainly by 'student approaches to learning' research. This research perspective developed in the early 1970s through the work of Marton and Säljö in Sweden, Biggs in Australia and Entwistle and Ramsden in the UK. This research, in line with other research in education and the social sciences more generally, moved away from a prescriptive search for laws of cause and effect in a laboratory situation to a search for explanations of the relationships between students and their actual higher education learning environments (Elton and Laurillard 1979).

This growing research into learning and teaching in higher education also impacted on the theories that are used to interpret learning and teaching situations. The texts from the 1970s cited earlier all drew on psychological theories developed outside of the context of learning in higher education. For example, Beard (1968) bemoaned the lack of an appropriate theory to help academics understand their teaching:

> Perhaps scientists whose subjects have a sound theoretical foundation do not feel at home with a subject which lacks a theory. For not only is there no theory to turn to when problems arise but theories of learning are too numerous and too little concerned with human learning to provide a framework for instruction.

> (Beard 1968: 1)

In recent works in higher education, theories of learning are more often, but certainly not always, taken as a starting point in this work. Prosser and Trigwell (1999: 10) build the argument in their book on a model for understanding learning and teaching in higher education that 'links aspects of the student's experiences of learning and the theoretical ideas derived from a phenomenographic perspective'. Phenomenography, which examines variation in the ways that a group of people experience a phenomenon, has built up from the work of Marton and Säljö (1976) and now has its own underpinning theory of learning (Marton and Booth 1997). Other approaches to researching student learning in higher education have also developed theories within a higher education context. For example the 'academic literacies' approach (Lea and Street 1998, Jones et al. 1999) has developed theories for thinking about students' writing in higher education.

Thus there has been a shift in focus from teaching techniques to the student experience in higher education, an increase in the amount of research, and an increase in the use of theory in thinking about learning and teaching in higher education. All of this has provided a stronger knowledge base for thinking about learning and teaching in higher education over the past 30 years and has played an important part in informing the changes that have taken place in learning and teaching in higher education.

The development of learning and teaching in higher education

The previous sections outlined changes in higher education that have, to some extent, driven the development of learning and teaching in higher education. We will now move to focus on the main subject of this book, which is an examination of how learning and teaching have developed. These developments will be examined in three different sections both in this chapter and in the book. These sections focus on the development of students' learning, the development of learning technologies and the development of teaching in higher education. Having outlined each of these sections, I will give a brief indication of what follows in the concluding chapter of this book.

Part I: The development of students' learning in higher education

As a result of the changes in the structure of higher education outlined above, there have been undoubted changes in the ways that students' learning has been supported and this is the focus of the second part of this book. As I indicated above, one of the major changes has been in terms of thinking about learning and teaching from the students' perspective, or in other words the development of a more 'learner-centred' approach. However, as David Boud indicates in Chapter 2, it is clear that 'learner-centred' has taken on a number of contradictory meanings over this time. Boud traces the development of the meaning of 'learner-centred' through a number of learning and teaching innovations that stretch from the early

1970s to the present day. Boud argues that the changing meaning of learner-centred indicates the changing position of learners within the discourses of learning and teaching in higher education. He argues that a more critical approach to learning and teaching is required that foregrounds the purposes of learning and views it within a broader context of social relations and power.

One of the key areas that David Boud identifies as a site of the exercise of uni-lateral power by academics over students is that of assessment. In Chapter 3, Vivien Hodgson examines students' experiences of participative assessment, which seeks to adopt a less hierarchical approach to assessing students' academic work with the aim of developing students as independent learners and critical thinkers. Hodgson reviews the literature on assessment and participative assessment before examining learners' experiences of participative assessment on a taught postgraduate course. Whilst she finds that participative assessment appears to encourage students to engage with the meaning of what they are learning, she identifies two different approaches that students appear to take to participative assessment: one is a more collective orientation and the other is a more individual orientation, which can lead to sterile and mechanistic transactions that do not ful-fil the promise of participative assessment. This provides a valuable warning that students' experiences of educational innovations are often different from those intended by the designers of such initiatives.

Chapter 4 shifts to consider postgraduate research students' experiences of learning. In this chapter, Pam Denicolo examines how understandings of the learning of research students have developed. Denicolo first examines changes in government policy relating to research students and then considers how this has impacted on the learning and teaching of postgraduate education. She indicates how institutions have developed their provision for research students and how the experience of a research student has broadened out from a single-minded focus on their particular project to focus on developing wider research skills across a range of methodologies. This has been accompanied by a shift from an apprenticeship model of supervision to one in which there is pressure for supervisors to be trained and one in which the quality of provision is under intense scrutiny.

In the last chapter of Part I, Will Bridge examines the changing relationships between the learning and teaching of non-traditional learners, in the sense of short-term or part-time students, and learning and teaching in the mainstream of higher education. This is placed in the context of changes in government policy relating to non-traditional students in higher education. He argues that non-traditional students are increasingly moving into the mainstream of higher educa-tion and that non-traditional students have played an important role in leading changes in learning and teaching that benefit all students in terms of flexible pro-vision and the importance of learning technologies. Bridge's focus on learning technology leads us nicely into Part II of this book which examines the develop-ment of learning technologies in higher education.

Part II: The development of learning technologies in higher education

There has been a revolution in learning technologies in higher education. This part of the book examines the development of e-learning in higher education and the conditions that are required for such learning to be successful.

In Chapter 6, Diana Laurillard examines the development of learning technologies since the 1970s and argues that whilst the rapid development of technologies has presented opportunities for the development of learning and teaching, these developments have never been driven by the needs of learners. She argues that the current focus of technology involves students in simply reading information rather than creating their own ideas and that what is required is a focus on how learning technology can support learning rather than new ways of learning being driven by what the technology can do.

In Chapter 7, David McConnell argues that the focus on technology has been too individualistic. He argues that in order to sustain student involvement in e-learning, we need to focus more on pedagogic designs which facilitate cooperative and collaborative e-learning opportunities. He argues that such designs allow students to construct meanings for themselves through engagement with others in an environment in which there is greater openness between teachers and students and in which students have a greater sense of being part of a community of learners.

Part III: The development of teaching in higher education

Part III of this book shifts to look at changes in the focus of the development of teaching in higher education. The Hale Report (UGC 1964) found that only 10 per cent of academics had been trained in teaching and bemoaned the lack of 'experiments' on teaching methods that had been carried out in the UK. They also reported that only four universities employed any staff to support teachers in developing their teaching. Since then there has been an explosion in the support for teaching, Gosling (2001) reporting that there were 84 educational development units amongst universities and colleges of higher education, which all had a remit to improve the quality of learning and teaching across their institutions. Seventy per cent of these were also responsible for organising postgraduate certificates in university teaching.

In Chapter 8, Liz Beaty examines the history of development of such accredited courses for teachers in higher education. As she argues, traditionally academics have seen themselves as educated in their discipline, through the apprenticeship of their PhDs, without considering the teaching of their discipline to be an area worthy of consideration. Beaty examines the development of accredited courses for university teachers, from the unaccredited courses that were largely for those who were interested in innovative teaching in the 1970s through to the current situation in which national professional standards for teaching are in the process of being developed that will inform a national accreditation framework.

Beyond the notion of an initial training in teaching is the idea that university academics might become scholars in teaching as well as in their disciplines. In Chapter 9, Lorraine Stefani examines the ways in which the scholarship of teaching is understood at different levels within higher education institutions, and considers the range and depth of pedagogical developments associated with the scholarship of learning and teaching. She also examines educational development as a scholarly activity and discusses what needs to be done in order for academics to take scholarship in their teaching as seriously as they take scholarship in their research.

Conclusions

The final chapter of this book seeks to make sense of what has gone before by thinking about the future of learning and teaching in higher education. It draws on the arguments in the previous chapters to offer two potential visions for higher education. In one vision, the concerns expressed in the earlier chapters are developed into a worse-case scenario and a bleak vision of the future is developed. In the other, the hopes of the authors are brought together in an optimistic vision of what learning and teaching in higher education might become. The purpose of this is not to suggest that either of these futures is likely; it is far more likely that a mixture of both will come to pass. Rather, it is to offer a sense of where the logic of different types of thinking about learning and teaching may take us. It is an argument for the careful consideration of the implications of changes in higher education on the experience of students and academics. For this book shows how little the experience of learning and teaching has been considered when changes have been made at all levels of higher education.

Notes

1 Based on Halsey's (1997) measure of dividing the number of full-time students by the number of full-time academic staff.

Part I

The development of students' learning in higher education

Chapter 2

'Aren't we all learner-centred now?'

The bittersweet flavour of success

David Boud

It is often remarked that one of the major changes in higher education over the second half of the twentieth century is that it has become more learner-centred. Indeed in the literature of teaching and learning a focus on the learner is so taken for granted that it is decreasingly commented on. This is summed up by the question in the title of this chapter 'aren't we all learner-centred now?' made recently by a student in a postgraduate education class. I'm not sure if it is true that we are all learner-centred, but, more worryingly, I'm not quite as sure what it means as I once was. To explore this question I wish to look back on the recent history of innovations aimed at supporting students' learning in higher education to see how we reached our present situation.

In 1969, I became the first full-time research student in the newly formed Institute for Educational Technology at the University of Surrey. Lewis Elton, who was then Professor of Physics, established the Institute as a vehicle for the pursuit of his long-standing interest in teaching and learning in higher education. As someone who had felt throughout school and university that what I had experienced as a student was not as good as it should have been, I relished the opportunity to make a contribution, not as a physics teacher, but as someone investigating the improvement of teaching and learning. My reforming tendencies on behalf of students could therefore be channelled in a productive direction. This began my formal interest in teaching and learning which has continued to the present. From the start, my perspective has been from that of the learner, recognising of course that the experience of the learner is mediated by what teachers do. In looking back over the years since then, it is apparent that what we took to be a learner focus is different from what we see now. At that time, almost every innovation that occurred was justified in terms of it being learner-centred. Today, learner-centred is a term that has become so commonplace, but still so desired, that it features centrally in national reports about higher education (National Committee of Inquiry into Higher Education 1997a) and in statements by government ministers (Nelson 2002).

The present universal discourse of higher education is that it should be centred on the learner. It has become an unquestioned mantra. Institutional texts and papers in the literature assume we know what we mean by learner-centred. However, this term means different things to different people who refer to different features of practice when they use it. We need to unpack these meanings if we are to prevent this term losing its particular value. In the past there was a question about whether being learner-centred might be too risky or too radical, but now it is assumed that all aspects of higher education should be learner-centred. However, this view disguises more than it reveals. Current views of learner-centred are in large part an unaware accretion of past conceptions. To understand where we are now we need to examine what went before. By appreciating the variations in the ways learner-centred has been used, we can develop a more nuanced understanding of how the discourse operates and reflect more critically on how terms are used. From this we will see that the idea of learner-centred contains a number of ideas, not a single one. Some of these ideas are not compatible with each other and herein lies a problem.

This chapter focuses on the changing ways in which the notion of 'learner-centred' has been used in undergraduate and postgraduate courses over the past 35 years or so. Rather than taking examples from the literature, I will take a partly autobiographical approach and illustrate the issues involved through examples of which I had direct personal experience and about which I published (mostly) contemporaneous accounts. Each example used represents a characteristic innovation of its time that was taken then to be focused on learners and learning. I shall examine what view of learner-centred is embodied in each and explore how this notion has changed over time. The aim of the chapter is to examine the different conceptions of learner-centred embedded in these innovations and the contributions they have made to understanding of the idea in order to reveal some of the problems that use of this term creates.

The innovations to be discussed are programmed learning and the Personalised System of Instruction (also known as the Keller Plan), self-directed and negotiated learning, problem-based learning and, finally, work-based learning. All these, in different ways, have been regarded as learner-centred. In universities today it is possible to see examples of most of these approaches in one form or another, though not necessarily in their original guise. Each of the selected ideas is described in the ways they were articulated at the time they became current. This is followed by observations of their particular features. How these emerge in one set of practices and are taken up in others is also noted.

Following the sequence of illustrations, I analyse them in terms of their conceptions of learner-centred. I discuss the implications for how we talk about learner-centredness today and suggest that perhaps this notion has outlived its usefulness and needs to be replaced by reference to what commentators are really referring to when they use the term. The question is posed: is there such a thing as learner-centred to which all can subscribe?

Learner-centred innovations

The obvious starting point is with students and their concerns. Prompted by the student reform movements of the late 1960s and the expressed dissatisfactions of students with their experience of higher education, moves were made throughout the western world to place students at the centre of consideration. This not only involved appointing them to university committees, but it also started to impinge on the ways courses were constructed and how they were taught. Changes to make higher education more student-centred gathered pace. The easiest immediate response to student dissatisfaction to accommodate was to highlight student choice of subject as a way of dealing with students' concerns. From the perspective of the twenty-first century this seems rather slight acknowledgment of students' volition; however, in the 1960s it was a major development. While mainstream higher education was focused on various forms of student choice, more substantial 'student-centred' innovations started to emerge.

Programmed learning and the Personalised System of Instruction

The key feature of programmed learning is the assumption that human beings can be efficiently programmed to learn. All that ultimately counts is that students should be able to demonstrate the required behaviour. The role of the designer of programmed learning – my first task on graduation – is to organise information in such a careful form that students cannot avoid learning (Skinner 1954, Schramm 1962). In programmed learning, students are not restricted in their learning by time or place. They control the rate of their study. Students may influence the pace of study, to a very limited extent the sequence of study and how long they might spend at any particular time. However, what they study is completely controlled by the programmer. Students study within a frame in which they have no part to play in what is to be learned other than their initial decision to undertake a course.

The learner-centred focus of programmed learning is on an unrelenting commitment to what students will do. If students do not learn it is the responsibility of the programmer to continually redesign the learning materials to ensure that they do and that they meet the criterion. This approach embodies the optimistic assumption that students can learn anything so long as it is presented to them in an appropriate manner. The important initiative of programmed learning was to free learners from the lock step of teachers' exposition. Students were not expected to go beyond the defined curriculum and there was no interest in them doing so.

The practical rather than conceptual limitation of programmed learning was that it involved a thorough analysis of the material to be learned and could not be realistically applied to the extent of material involved in any given course module. It also involved a shift of responsibility away from the teacher to the instructional designer and challenged the cultural practices of educational institutions. While there would always be a demand for the kind of learner-centredness of programmed learning, it remained contained in lower level vocational training or confined to the domain of those working with computer assisted learning. The impact on the higher education mainstream was minor.

However, the possibilities opened up by a behavioural approach led to a search for further innovation. This was represented by what was probably the first large-scale learning-oriented innovation in higher education that took account of behavioural science. Known familiarly as the Keller plan, after its founder Fred Keller, or more formally as the Personalised System of Instruction (PSI), it took from programmed learning the idea of mastery. That is, all students could achieve the highest level of performance (mastery) if the conditions of their learning could be sufficiently well controlled. There was uptake in psychology, particularly in the United States, and in the physical sciences. Lewis Elton was the principal figure who introduced PSI in the sciences to the UK.

> In a Keller plan course, students work on their own, at their own pace (Keller 1968: 79). Lectures are not used as the main method of teaching, although a few are provided for interest and stimulation. The course material is divided into units, each representing about one week's work. For each unit, the student is provided with written material, which states the objectives to be reached by the end of the unit and suggests means of achieving them, e.g. he [sic] may be asked to read certain pages of a textbook, read additional notes provided which discuss the topic, and do certain given problems. When he feels he has mastered the unit, he takes a short (20 minute) test. Immediately after the test, a tutor discusses his results with him and can give guidance based on the particular problems that have emerged. If the student passes, he goes on to the next unit: if he fails, he must do more work on the unit and then try again. Failure on unit tests does not affect his final assessment in any way.
>
> (Elton *et al.* 1973: 164)

The Keller plan can be seen as introducing key ideas of behaviourism into the day-to-day realities of the university course. However, it acknowledges that it is not practicable to programme all that is required for university study. It utilises the key idea of mastery to indicate to students that they can achieve all that is required of them. Human intervention takes place through individual discussion between tutors and students following a test in which their learning difficulties are diagnosed. Students progress rapidly or slowly through such courses depending on how much assistance they require. Tutors spend most time with students who require them most.

The Keller Plan provided a major challenge to the conventional assumption that it was necessary for all students to be extended, and therefore for most to fail to learn, rather than that all students should be brought to mastery. A major concern was that the Keller Plan placed emphasis on the least able students rather than challenging the more able ones. This was an important learner-centred shift as it exposed, on a weekly basis, what students had actually learned and brought this starkly to the attention of teachers. It also shifted the discourse from what teachers did to what students do through a focus on specified achievable learning outcomes, the provision of learning materials and frequent tests.

The uptake of the Keller Plan was predominantly in subject areas involving demanding sequential content matter where ideas necessarily built closely on those that had gone before, such as calculus, mechanics and behavioural psychology. It was also taken up in areas in which teachers were prepared to make the substantial investment of time to document their courses in great detail and provide rich materials and multiple test items. However, one of the reasons for its success was that it was capable of fitting within the resource and timetabling constraints of university courses (Boud *et al.* 1975). Learner-centredness focused on ensuring that students could reliably and confidently meet the learning objectives specified. The trade-off for this achievement was a narrowing of focus on to the necessary and core ideas of programmes and courses. There was little or no student choice other than the decision to enrol. That was the price to be paid for mastery.

Self-directed learning/negotiated learning

In its broadest meaning, 'self-directed learning' describes a process in which individuals take the initiative, with or without the help of others, in diagnosing their learning needs, formulating learning goals, identifying human and material resources for learning, choosing and implementing appropriate learning strategies, and evaluating learning outcomes. Other labels found in the literature to describe this process are 'self-planned learning', 'inquiry method', 'independent learning', 'self-education', 'self-instruction', 'self-teaching', 'self-study', and 'autonomous learning'. The trouble with most of these labels is that they seem to imply learning in isolation, whereas self-directed learning usually takes place in association with various kinds of helpers, such as teachers, tutors, mentors, resource people, and peers. There is a lot of mutuality among a group of self-directed learners.

(Knowles 1975: 18)

Self-directed learning represented a radical departure from the behaviourism of programmed learning and the Keller Plan. Based on a humanist philosophy that placed learners' desires as central, self-directed learning provided a means by which learners' own projects could be encompassed within educational courses. In contrast to the Keller Plan in which the teacher defined the goals and the programme, and allowed students choice only of pace, self-directed learning placed the selection of learning goals and programmes in the hands of students and positioned teachers as responding to these. There was an uneasy relationship between self-directed learning practices and conventional defined curricula. Students might not choose to study that which was expected of them. Negotiating unique programmes of study with each student was necessarily time consuming.

One of the principal vehicles proposed by Knowles to pursue self-directed learning was the learning contract, and in later years learning contracts and self-directed learning became almost synonymous (Knowles and Associates 1986). A learning contract is a document used to assist in the planning and monitoring of a learning project.

> A learning contract is essentially an agreement negotiated between a learner and a staff adviser that certain activities will be undertaken in order to achieve particular learning goals and that specific evidence will be produced to demonstrate the goals have been reached. In return, formal recognition (often in the form of academic credit) is given for the work produced.
>
> From the outset, the learner is encouraged to identify his or her own learning needs and to develop learning objectives and strategies consistent with those needs. ...
>
> The contract serves as both a statement of intended outcomes and a plan of action, listing both the learning objectives and the means of achieving them. The exact form it takes is subject to negotiation. The contract must in principle and practice be open to renegotiation. For instance, if a learner wishes to change emphasis or redesign the original objectives. This feature means that contracts are flexible and learner-centred not only in terms of initial conceptions of a topic but can respond to changed learner's awareness.
>
> (Anderson and Boud 1996)

The radical focus of student choice of content provided a natural limit to the uptake of these ideas. However, variations of learning contracts were widely used (Anderson *et al.* 1998). These involved, for example, teachers specifying a proportion of the outcomes in advance as a non-negotiable component and the use of Knowles's idea of students self-diagnosing their own competencies as a starting point.

Following the articulation of this practice in 1975 by Malcolm Knowles in his book *Self-Directed Learning: A Guide for Learners and Teachers*, the use of learning contracts was associated with Knowles's term 'self-directed learning'. Subsequently, this term has been less frequently used and 'negotiated learning' advocated (e.g. Anderson *et al.* 1996) in recognition that in any system in which individual learning is assessed and accredited there are limits to self-direction. Negotiation implies that there are some aspects of a learning plan that may not be negotiable by either party.

Self-directed learning has been used widely in higher education in areas such as education and the health sciences. The device of learning contracts has been taken up extensively in many areas in which student projects are common as it provides a way of managing this aspect of the curriculum. It has also been used as a frame for work placements and practical activities in which there is typically less direct teacher control over what is to be learned than in conventional coursework.

Problem-based learning

The principal idea behind problem-based learning is ... that the starting point for learning should be a problem, a query or a puzzle that the learner wishes to solve.

(Boud 1985: 13)

Problem-based learning is a way of constructing and teaching courses using problems as the stimulus and focus for student activity ... It is a way of conceiving of the curriculum as being centred upon key problems in professional practice. Problem-based courses start with problems rather than with exposition of disciplinary knowledge.

... The following features are characteristic of problem-based learning:

- using stimulus material to help students discuss an important problem, question or issue;
- presenting the problem as a simulation of professional practice or a 'real life' situation;
- appropriately guiding students' critical thinking and providing limited resources to help them learn from defining and attempting to resolve the given problem;
- having students work cooperatively as a group, exploring information in and out of class, with access to a tutor (not necessarily a subject specialist) who knows the problem well and can facilitate the group's learning process;
- getting students to identify their own learning needs and appropriate use of available resources;
- reapplying this new knowledge to the original problem and evaluating their learning processes.

(Boud and Feletti 1997: 1–2)

Problem-based learning was the first major attempt to adopt a student-centred approach in areas with professional requirements and very substantial bodies of knowledge to be learned. The emphasis in problem-based learning is on equipping students to be effective self-directed learners within their professional domain. This occurs through constructing an entire curriculum as a form of learning-to-learn within the profession. While all activities aim to extend and develop professional knowledge, they also require students to work with others to identify what they need to know and how to approach new problems. The focus is on learners working collaboratively with other learners, so the emphasis is not just on independent learning but on interdependent learning and thus on the ability to learn with others. Unlike conventional professional curricula the emphasis from the start is on students identifying and defining problems rather than on the provision of disciplinary information. The sequence of problems posed to students is normally given but within each sequence students have substantial scope for deciding their own approach.

Of all the innovations mentioned so far, problem-based learning has had the most extensive impact on practice and there are hundreds of major programmes in a variety of professions throughout the world that are problem-based. In the area of medicine, for example, there are many examples of high-status medical schools that have taken a problem-based focus (e.g. Harvard, Sydney). Problem-based learning illustrates that a learner-centred view is not incompatible with training for knowledge-rich high-risk professions.

Unlike the behaviourism of programmed learning, or the humanism of self-directed learning, problem-based learning is based upon constructivism. That is, the idea that knowledge is constructed by learners. In such a view, students need opportunities to practise the identification and formulation of the knowledge they require for different purposes. Constructivism includes the idea that individuals construct their own knowledge, but also that knowledge is socially constructed. Both these ideas are embodied in the collaborative approach to problem definition and solution within problem-based learning which aims to mirror the way knowledge is generated within professional practice.

Work-based learning

Work-based learning takes a radical approach to the notion of a university education as students undertake study for a degree or diploma through activities conducted primarily in their workplace and in topic areas in which there may be no immediate equivalence with university subjects. ... Learning opportunities are not contrived for study purposes, but arise from normal work. ... Work is not a discrete and limited element of study; it is the foundation of the curriculum.

(Boud 1998)

Work-based learning programmes typically share the following characteristics:

1   A partnership between an external organization and an educational institution is specifically established to foster learning.
2   Learners negotiate learning plans approved by representatives of both the educational institution and the organization. Different learners follow quite different pathways.
3   The programme followed derives from the needs of the workplace and of the learner rather than being controlled or framed by the disciplinary or professional curriculum.
4   The starting point and educational level of the programme is established after a process of recognition of current competencies and identification of the learning in which they wish to engage.
5   Learning projects are undertaken in the workplace. These are oriented to the challenges of work and the future needs of the learner and the organization.

6   The educational institution assesses the learning outcomes of the negoti-
     ated programmes with respect to a framework of standards and levels.

(Boud *et al.* 2001: 4–7)

In the other innovations discussed so far, ultimate control of what is to be learned
has been configured in terms of a given curriculum. This is the case even in self-
directed learning where considerable scope is available for students to define their
own programme. Work-based learning, in contrast, starts with the assumption that
the activities of learners outside the educational institution provide not just the
starting point but the whole *raison d'être* of learning. The role of staff is to
respond directly to the needs of students and their workplaces and to act as a
learning broker between learners and their workplace. Work-based learning is
learner-centred in the same respect as negotiated learning, but with the expectation that some of the possible degrees of freedom available are circumscribed by
the exigencies of work.

To be formally recognised, the resulting learning ultimately needs to be judged
against a framework of academic assessment standards and levels. However, in
work-based learning, this framework is specifically designed to recognise knowledge beyond that conventionally dealt with within the educational institution.
Work-based learning is therefore learner-centred with respect to goals, programme of activity, knowledge requirements and performance. In some respects,
therefore, it could be seen to be the culmination of the learner-centred agenda.
That this might not be realised in practice is more a function of the relationships
between the learner and their employing organisation than with the university.

Work-based learning in comparison with some of the other innovations discussed here has, as yet, influenced universities to a limited extent. Nevertheless, it
is now part of universities' responses to new learning demands within the trans-
disciplinary learning world of work. It provides a way of engaging with
knowledge that does not fit within the traditional boundaries of disciplines and
professions.

Discussion

What do these examples reveal about changing views of learner-centredness? The
practices described provide well-documented examples of teaching and learning
in higher education that enable us to focus on the changing positioning of learners
within the discourse of teaching and learning. They indicate differences in underlying philosophical and psychological assumptions, a differing focus on methods
or practices, and differing representations of learner power.

Underlying philosophy of teaching and learning

While there have never been very obvious connections in higher education
between teaching and learning and particular philosophical or psychological

views, such views have been influential on the various ideas that have been taken up. Programmed learning and the Keller Plan were based on ideas from behavioural psychology that emphasised that all learners could achieve, so long as the conditions were right and enough time was given. Self-directed learning was based on ideas of humanistic psychology articulated by Carl Rogers (1969) and others, arising out of a client-centred focus to education and psychology. Self-directed learning exemplified the humanistic features of commitment to student decision-making and freedom to learn. In self-directed learning, what was to be learned was subordinated to the greater importance of student initiation of learning and programmes formulated by students in response to their desires and self-diagnosed needs. There was much emphasis given to the formulation of learning plans in the literature on self-directed learning, but relatively little given to their execution. This arose from their focus on a deep respect for the learner and a subordination of teaching to their expressed needs.

In contrast, there is close attention to learning processes in problem-based learning and an emphasis on learning to be an effective professional learner. The underpinning philosophy of constructivism is apparent through the use of problems to prompt learners to engage deeply with subject matter to address the problem so as to make knowledge their own. The philosophical foundations of work-based learning, whilst sharing some common threads with problem-based learning and self-directed learning, come from a re-appraisal of what constitutes legitimate knowledge and a questioning of universities' control over it. In some respects it is post-modern in that it questions the canon of academic discourse. In other respects it is very modernistic in that it assumes that there is such a notion as 'working knowledge' which can be learned and enhanced.

So, there is no common set of philosophical or psychological ideas that underlies this variety of innovation. There are clusters of compatibility around behaviourism or humanism and, at the micro level, constructivism may influence the conduct of negotiated learning or work-based learning activities. Indeed, there are fundamental contradictions between the ideas on which the practices draw. For example, behavioural approaches focus on the performance of tasks and do not aim to promote the construction of knowledge beyond the instrumental. It is not possible to discern shared foundations for the diverse set of learner-centred approaches, and incompatibilities are evident. The central feature of self-direction of negotiated learning is, for example, relegated to a single student decision about pace of learning for those involved in mastery learning.

The centrality of the learner

There has been a move away from thinking that there could be teaching methods that in themselves address educational problems, to recognition that it is not 'methods' that determine what students learn. It is now accepted that no matter how we use and interpret methods, it is the actual learning experiences learners have and how they interpret them that determine their learning outcomes. That said, we should still acknowledge the seductive qualities of an all-encompassing method that seeks to encompass new ways of promoting learning and new kinds of outcomes. The power of the discourse of new educational practices will remain even when particular versions of them – as we have seen with programmed learning – disappear.

The learner-centred discourse constructs the learner at the centre of teaching and learning activity. This positioning of the iconic learner by others occurs partly as a reaction against earlier positioning of the teacher at the centre. The learner-centred discourse created an alternative centre and generated a conceptual battle about whose perspective should reign. This way of looking at things created an inappropriate polarity and a vying of position between teachers and learners. It focused on a particular dimension of teaching and learning to the exclusion of others, i.e. whose concerns are dominant, the teacher or the learner? The discursive strategy of focusing attention on learners was by no means an unreasonable move given their previous neglect. However, an excess of attention to this dimension can draw attention away from many other potentially important concerns such as the total learning environment, emotional and cultural demands on students, or, indeed, what we are seeking to produce. There are still many examples of conventional teaching practice that inappropriately privilege teachers' perspectives, and the battle may still need to be engaged at the local level. However, this does not mean that in terms of future development this is the most important issue with which to be concerned.

This centre-periphery model assumes that there is a teacher or a learner, or perhaps a generic teacher or learner, that occupies a particular position. It may, however, be more fruitful to recognise that there is not one centre and one periphery, but many. The process of learning is always one in which learners move from the periphery of knowledge to a state of becoming closer to knowledge they have not yet acquired. So perhaps we should de-centre learner-centredness and recognise that learners are always in a state of becoming. Sometimes they are aspiring to the knowledge of their teachers, sometimes they are not.

We know from extensive research on student learning that we must take a relational view of learning and see it from the perspective of the learner at least as much as from the perspective of the teacher (Ramsden 1987). Learners in one sense always see themselves at the centre of their world, but in another sense see themselves on the periphery of worlds they wish to access. A learner-centred perspective now perhaps involves recognising this multi-positioned view of the learner and needs to develop models and discourses that respond to it. These will not be based on a simple polarity between teachers and learners and naive privileging of those whose concerns are paramount. Neither will it be based on a unitary view of a centre to which learners necessarily aspire.

Learner-centredness and power

One of the ways in which learner-centredness was discussed in the 1970s and early 1980s was in terms of student control. To be student-centred was to provide opportunities for students to control increasing aspects of their learning. In programmed learning and the Keller Plan this focused on giving students control of pace and thus self-paced learning was a term often used to describe these approaches. Later, the use of learning contracts focused attention on students making decisions about their learning objectives, their programme of study and their outcomes. We can see a kind of educational progressivism opening up the different dimensions that learners could control. This was superseded by the idea that in most circumstances it is not the formal degree of control that is important for students but meaningful control within the context in which they operate. That is, if pace is not what is significant for students then self-pacing will not be experienced as learner-centred. So, for example, a student seeking to become a doctor would not want to exert decisions about every aspect of the curriculum, but they would expect to influence those aspects that relate to becoming more effective in their professional practice. The absolute idea of student control was replaced by the relativism of influence within contexts.

One of the ironies of writing about learner-centredness through examples of teaching practice is that these define learner-centred from the point of view of the teacher or designer of educational programmes. Whether or not any given student experiences something as learner-centred, or centred on his or her own needs and interests, involves a quite different discussion. A fuller account of changes in learner-centredness would necessarily take the conceptions of learners into account. However, ignoring this here does not invalidate our discussion as university courses have been defined and developed, by and large, by teachers for teachers. As we have seen in some approaches, e.g. self-directed learning and work-based learning, there are areas of activity in which learners can exert much more substantial control. Nevertheless, these are, and will probably remain, in the minority at least at the undergraduate level.

Until the 1980s we saw that different models embodied the idea that freedom to learn (Rogers 1969) should necessarily increase. Later models moved away from a simple focus on increased freedom towards a learner-centred approach that takes into account the purposes of learning (Boud 1987). Thus we see problem-based learning and work-based learning as illustrating ways in which teaching and learning activities can more closely correspond to the exigencies of professional practice and the workplace. So, rather than viewing learning as involving more freedom, these models do not articulate their key features in terms of freedoms, but in terms of fitness for their varying purposes.

The shift away from striving to have student control is reflected in changing conceptions of power through this period. The older idea of power as possessed by one person and only able to be shared by others has been replaced by a more discursive view that all parties have power and they exercise it in different ways. Power is now seen as productive and circulating, not something simply possessed by individuals or institutions (Gore 1995, Brookfield 2001). Power is not a zero sum game to be shifted from teacher to student; it is able to be exercised through influence or resistance at all times. Therefore the goal was not to move it from teachers to students but to recognise ways in which it was exercised within different teaching and learning practices. So for example, in early examples of self-directed learning there was a pretence that students could choose whatever they wanted and other parties to the contract would broadly accept this. This view was later replaced by the recognition that learning contracts involved negotiation between two parties with different interests, and this necessarily meant that some things were open to negotiation and others were not. This recognition enabled both parties to exercise power over aspects that they valued. The ways in which this was done naturally varied from situation to situation.

The one area in which power continues to be unilaterally exercised by teachers is in the area of assessment, which is discussed in more detail by Vivien Hodgson in Chapter 3. While many of the innovations discussed involved students testing themselves or engaging in various forms of self-assessment (Boud 1995), ultimately sovereign power of teachers resided in their ultimate control over assessment. In some cases this rendered student control over other aspects of the curriculum illusory. Even today, it is possible to find bold aspirational language about student-centredness within courses circumscribed by oppressive assessment practices.

Acknowledging that power is everywhere and is productive does not mean, however, that we can forgo examination of educational practices in terms of intrinsic features that inhibit or enhance opportunities for students to make decisions. Courses can still be designed in ways that proscribe student involvement in decisions about what is studied, how it is studied and how it is assessed. Students may exercise their power through resisting such programmes but this creates a very different environment to one in which students are able to direct their energies elsewhere. In this, the structure of the programme may not matter any more. We have come to recognise that the use of power is not determined by the structure of the programme; nevertheless, the structure of programmes is still important in influencing students' responses and in directing their energy productively or otherwise.

Concluding remarks

It can be seen that although the various approaches discussed have a strong focus on the learner, they do so in quite different ways. They draw upon different sets of ideas from different traditions. They cannot be collapsed into a single view. When someone uses the term 'learner-centred' now, we must ask ourselves: what is it that is being referred to? Which set of ideas or practices is meant? Are some being rejected whilst others are accepted? What is a learner focus being used to represent?

We have passed the point at which we can use this language as if we knew what was being referred to. We must ask the harder question: what is this language seeking to achieve? What is being privileged and what is being ignored? It is through a more critical approach to how we refer to teaching and learning practices that we will be able to operate more effectively. It is time perhaps to move away from an exclusive focus on learner-centredness to viewing teaching and learning within its broader context and network of social relations. The purpose of learning needs to be placed in the foreground along with the processes involved in addressing those purposes. By making these explicit, ironically, we may yet reach a wider appreciation of what learner-centred might mean.

Note

'Student' and 'learner' are used as interchangeable here as all the learners referred to are students. Learner has become more popular in recent years as a way of encompassing those who may not have the formal status of students enrolled in an educational institution.

Chapter 3

Participative assessment and the learners' experience

Vivien Hodgson

Introduction

In this chapter I would like to examine the differences between conventional assessment practices and participative assessment in terms of the pedagogical assumption associated with participative assessment but also, more specifically, from the point of view of the learners' experience. As I will discuss in more detail below, assessment requirements have frequently been shown to be an important influence on the approach that learners adopt to learning within conventional higher education courses and programmes. However, learners' experience of participative assessment within the context of learner-centred or less traditional courses has not been studied to the same extent. Whether or not their experience of participative assessment influences their learning approach in similar ways as for some learners within the context of more traditional courses has not really been considered.

I will first describe what I mean by assessment and how it is frequently viewed by policy makers, educational researchers and learners themselves. I will then introduce participative assessment and how it has emerged as an important idea associated with particularly learner-centred approaches within higher education. I will describe what are seen to be the advantages of adopting participative assessment approaches as well as some of the potential problems that have been identified by various authors. Finally, I will describe some studies that have attempted to look specifically at the learners' experience of participative assessment.

Assessment in higher education

Assessment in higher education is essentially a process of judging someone's understanding (Entwistle and Entwistle 1997). Entwistle claims that the most usual way of judging understanding is through what Perkins and Blythe (1994) describe as 'understanding performances'.

It remains the case that academic staff will generally make the decision on whether or not understanding has been demonstrated, most often by judging students' performances when either answering examination questions or when writing essay answers on topics or questions assigned to them by their teachers/assessors.

Lewis Elton has long been a critic of dominant assessment practices and in a review of assessment research commented that:

> Traditional assessment practices, consisting pre-eminently of the assessment of essay and problem type final examinations and similarly constructed coursework, cannot adequately test for imponderables like independent critical thinking, creativity etc, and this is particularly so for time limited examinations.
>
> (Elton and Johnston 2002: 7)

In addition, as Reynolds and Trehan (2000) reiterated, with the ultimate function of assessment in higher education being to provide the basis for granting or withholding qualifications, this makes it a primary location for power relations. Despite this the practices and processes involved in assessment are seldom considered in any depth when designing courses or when looking at the learners' experience of learning and of assessment itself. It was recognition of the hierarchical and authoritarian nature of assessment practices that originally led people like Heron (1981), amongst others, to seek to move away from a position where tutors exercise unilateral, intellectual authority and to move towards more participative assessment approaches that actively involve the people who are being judged.

McConnell (2002b) claimed recently that the case for participative forms of assessment has by now been well made. Whilst various authors may focus on slightly different forms of participative assessment and variously describe them as peer assessment, collaborative and/or consultative assessment etc., they all refer to forms of assessment that seek to directly involve and share the responsibility for assessment with learners.

The case for using participative forms of assessment has been made primarily on pedagogical principles that believe it is important to adopt less hierarchical, more participative and 'learner-centred' teaching and learning approaches. McConnell explains, 'collaborative assessment seeks to foster a learning approach to assessment'. (McConnell 2002b). In addition, as Boud (1986) claimed earlier, peer assessment helps to develop independent learners and critical thinkers. Indeed Falchikov (1995) found, in a study of peer assessment which emphasised the giving of critical feedback as well as awarding a grade, that student learning by means of reflection, analysis and diplomatic criticism was enhanced.

It could be argued that participative assessment approaches are an important potential tool to be used by universities when seeking to offer students the kind of learning experiences that Laurillard, in Chapter 6, claims will be necessary if they are to produce employees who are intellectually confident, and able to take responsibility for their personal development of knowledge and skills. This is an aspiration for higher education that has been highlighted in a number of policy documents and initiatives in recent years including the White Paper *The Future of Higher Education* (DfES 2003a) and in the Higher Education Funding Council for England (HEFCE) *Strategic Plan 2003–2008* (updated April 2004) following the White Paper. The potential contribution of assessment practices has not gone unrecognised, as HEFCE states in its strategic plan:

> Good teaching includes effective assessment of learning. We are encouraging assessment that helps learners to understand their developing strengths and makes visible the value added through their studies.
>
> (HEFCE 2004: 18)

In the main, the preferred proposed option for change to assessment practices appears to be the development of an assessment portfolio approach. Indeed, Lewis Elton is an advocate of such an approach and has produced for the LTSN Generic Centre, now the Higher Education Academy, a paper entitled *Seven Pillars of Assessment Wisdom* (Elton 2003) that outlines some key principles for adopting such an approach.

Elton clearly believes that participative/peer assessment has an important part to play within an assessment portfolio approach and whilst it is by no means seen as the linchpin, it is nonetheless seen as an important potential component. As Elton and Johnston comment in their comprehensive review of assessment practices:

> This makes it possible to use less costly and possibly less reliable methods, including self and peer assessment. One can then go on from there to the assessment of skills, such as group skills where self and peer assessment may be the only possible form even summatively, and mental skills, such as criticality, where the development of the skill and its assessment cannot sensibly be divorced from each other.
>
> (Elton and Johnston 2002: 15)

David McConnell, in Chapter 7, describes a study that he carried out into the learners' experience of networked collaborative assessment. The study did, in his view, demonstrate that participative assessment was an important learning process in its own right and one that did contribute to the development of skills that could be transferred to other lifelong learning situations and contexts. However, he does acknowledge that it is not without its difficulties and that it is, for example, important to foster a trusting relationship amongst all involved in order for it to succeed.

In his study, however, McConnell did not consider to any great extent how the learner's experience of participative assessment is either different from or similar to that reported in studies of the learner's experience of assessment in more conventional processes and models of assessment. As I will presently outline, studies of learners' experience in more conventional courses have shown assessment to be both a significant and important influence upon learners' experience of learning and can lead to differences in learners' approach to learning as well as to learning outcomes. Whether assessment has a similar or different impact on learners' experiences of participative assessment is something I will explore in this chapter.

In addition, it is beginning to be increasingly acknowledged that the processes through which participative assessment achieves the many aspirations and claims made cannot be assumed to be unproblematic. As already mentioned, McConnell notes the importance of developing a trusting relationship between those involved. Reynolds and Trehan (2000) go further and make the case for a more critical examination of the processes and power relations that are involved. Consequently, this is something I will also consider in more detail in this chapter.

The significance of assessment upon learners' experience

That students' perceptions and experience of academic assessment practices and demands are a key influence upon their lives as students and their approach to their studies has long been recognised. Early studies such as *Making the Grade* (Becker *et al.* 1968), *The Hidden Curriculum* (Snyder 1971) and *Degrees of Excellence* (Entwistle and Wilson 1977) alerted the educational world to how pervasive an influence assessment was on the experience of students. In *Up to the Mark*, Miller and Parlett (1974) revealed in more depth the different approaches students took to dealing with assessment. They identified students who adopted a pro-active 'cue seeking' approach, through to those who were 'cue conscious' and recognised that it was necessary to be alert to what was expected in given assessment situations. Finally, they claimed that some students could be described as 'cue deaf' and unable to discern that in order to succeed academically it was important to be strategic in their approach to assessment.

In the 1980s, research on the learner's experience and approach to learning similarly confirmed the significance of assessment on learners' approach to learning. In particular, researchers identified what they described as a 'strategic approach' to learning, where the intention is to achieve the highest possible grades by using organised study methods and good time-management (Ramsden and Entwistle 1981, Biggs 1978). Since then, strategic approaches to learning have been reported to include such things as monitoring one's study effectiveness (Entwistle *et al.* 2000) and an awareness of the assessment process, aspects which are akin to metacognitive alertness and regulation (Vermunt 1998). Interviews with students who adopt a strategic approach suggest that they have two specific foci of concern – the academic content of the system (which is fairly typical of a 'deep approach' as described by Marton and Säljö 1976), coupled with the demands of the assessment system (usually associated with a 'surface approach' also described by Marton and Säljö 1976).

In similar vein, Gibbs *et al.* (1984) suggested students have different educational orientations and that students can have what they describe as a personal educational orientation to their work. They claimed a personal educational orientation was most often associated with deep learning. On the other hand, students can have what they describe as a 'reproducing' orientation where they are more influenced by fear of failure or other extrinsic factors, such as passing exams. This orientation is most associated with adopting a surface approach to learning with an emphasis on rote learning and recall and, as a consequence, surface-level learning. Gibbs *et al.* believe that students can also have a third educational orientation which they also describe as strategic. Students that adopt a strategic orientation are more competitive and achievement related but also, they claim, it is an orientation that has the potential to be associated with deep-level learning.

In summary, studies of learners' experience and educational orientation suggest that the way students experience and approach assessment has an influence on learning outcomes. For some students this can be an essentially negative influence leading to surface approaches to learning and surface-level learning outcomes. On the other hand students can adopt a 'strategic approach' to their studies which allows them to both meet the demands of assessment and achieve academic success as well as deep-level learning outcomes. It is important to note that, as explained by several authors, neither educational orientation nor learning approach are considered to be fixed attributes of an individual learner. Laurillard (1997) explains that the deep/surface dichotomy does not characterise a stable characteristic of a student, but rather describes a relationship between the student's perceptions of a task and his or her approach to it. The organisational framework and/or context in which learning is carried out and how it is handled or managed is likely to impact on both the learning experience and the adopted learning approach. Hence it will also impact on the learning outcome. This has been confirmed in studies, such as Nuy (1991) and Dart and Clarke (1991).

Participative assessment within learner-centred courses

The studies mentioned so far, which have highlighted the importance of assessment and how learners' experience of assessment demands is likely to influence learning outcomes, have all been carried out in the context of essentially conventional education contexts or situations. The assessment practices involved have equally been conventional ones and have been entirely the responsibility of academic staff. They have not considered the way assessment is experienced within more participative learner-centred educational designs and ones that include participative assessment as part of those designs.

It has long been recognised that assessment remains a pervasive influence upon learners' experience within such learning contexts and that there is a difficult tension between the concept and ideas underpinning participative and learning-centred approaches and the concept and idea of assessing the performance of others. As

Heron (1981) pointed out, generally speaking, tutors exercise unilateral, intellectual authority in assessment even in otherwise learner-centred courses.

Hodgson and Reynolds, in an early study of the learner's experience of the dynamics of the learning community, commented:

> So for example although the intention was to transform the tutor–student relationship within the programme, ultimate control over assessment mitigated against this. Tutors were seen both as traditional authority figures and, on occasions, as failing to exercise their authority.
>
> (Hodgson and Reynolds 1987: 155)

In the programme that they studied, like other programmes seeking to be more participative at that time, Hodgson and Reynolds go on to explain that corresponding changes to the assessment system were consequently introduced;

> The assessment procedure was made more collaborative in an attempt to bridge the constraints and expectations of the academic community and more democratic philosophy of the course design.
>
> (Hodgson and Reynolds 1987: 157)

It is not, however, always the case in learner-centred designs that participative assessment follows. David Boud points out in Chapter 2 that it is not teaching methods per se that determine what students learn. As he explains, it is now accepted that no matter how we use and interpret the methods, it is the actual learning experiences that learners have that determine students' learning outcomes. As he goes on to point out, whilst there are now many more teaching methods and designs that are intended to be learner-centred, the area over which teachers continue to exercise unilateral power is that of assessment. He makes the point that, ultimately, teachers retain sovereign power within the teaching and learning situation due to their ultimate control over assessment.

Where changes to more participative methods have occurred, as Reynolds and Trehan (2000) imply when writing about assessment practices within critical management studies, assessment as the embodiment of institutional power is not necessarily acknowledged by those involved, as they explain:

> Yet while examples of critical pedagogy are accumulating, they seldom reflect corresponding change in assessment practices. Where assessment does depart from mainstream practice, alternatives are typically based on humanistic, student centered aspirations for social equality, rather than an analysis of the assessment process in terms of institutional power.
>
> (Reynolds and Trehan 2001: 268)

Mann (2001) goes further and makes the point that two key technologies of power in the modern world, identified by Foucault (1979), of examination and confession are clearly highly relevant to all assessment practices including those normally associated with learner-centred designs. As she explains:

> The examination, by making the individual visible, objectifies and individualises, where as confession subjectifies, drawing more of the person into the domain of power. Confession takes place in conversations in which there is a speaker (the learner) and an Other who listens, judges, has the power to forgive, and who crucially requires the confession in the first place. Educational practices such as learning journals, profiles and learning contracts could all be said to be examples of the technology of power of confession.
>
> (Mann 2001: 14)

Boud in Chapter 2 clearly acknowledges the influence and relevance of power within the experience of assessment practices but goes on to state that whilst we should seek to avoid oppressive assessment practices it is still important to assess learning. Boud suggests that the structure of a given programme, including opportunities to involve students in decisions about what is studied and how it is assessed, does not determine either the experience or location of power within it. It does, he suggests, nonetheless remain an important influence on students' experience and whether their energies are directed productively or not.

Writers such as Boud have long argued that participative assessment methods are more compatible with the philosophy and intentions of learner-centred education and, by implication, are considered one of the structures within an educational programme that can positively impact on the learners' 'energy productivity'. Whether this is the case for all learners or whether the institutional power invested in any assessment process is experienced by some in ways that result in them still adopting a surface approach to learning will only be revealed through studies of learners' experiences of participative assessment in practice.

How participative assessment practices within the structure of a given programme designed to support a participative learning community design and approach is experienced by learners will be examined in the next section.

Learner experience of participative assessment processes and practice

For many years the MA in Management Learning, now the MA in Management Learning and Leadership (Mamll), at Lancaster University Management School has included a form of participative assessment. The MA is for professionals working in the field of management development or education as well as for managers with an interest in learning and development. It is a two-year part-time masters' programme with three one-week residentials each year. Between the workshops the course participants meet in tutor groups, known as learning sets, of four to six learners plus a tutor per set. The learning sets meet either online, via computer mediated discussion spaces, or face to face, according to the set members' preferences. Mamll has an open syllabus and participants are encouraged to work as a learning community and to take responsibility for the content and design of the course within the broad field of management learning. Assessment is participative in that the choice of topic for all assignments is discussed and decided within the learning sets. The learning sets' members advise each other on their assignments, read each other's completed work and participate in a feedback and marking meeting for each other's assignments, all in consultation with the set tutor.

In between the residential workshops the course is supported by a networked learning environment that allows participants to continue interacting virtually with each other both generally and, more specifically, with their learning sets. In addition, the environment offers access to a range of resources and information. In designing the environment there was an assumption that it would support and extend the idea of learners joining a 'knowledge community', in this case the knowledge community of management learning. (Hodgson and Zenios 2003). The networked learning environment was thus not intended to be a place to examine performance as such but a place where learners could not only find information but, more importantly, participate in learning dialogues with peers. It is, however, also the place where participants can choose to do their work for course assignments and carry out the process of participative assessment that is practised on the MA.

A series of small-scale phenomenographic studies (Asensio *et al.* 2000, Hodgson and Zenios 2003, Hodgson and Watland 2004) have found that in practice participants' experience of using the networked learning environment is mostly related to what they need to do or be involved in for assessment purposes.

For example, Hodgson and Zenios concluded, after a series of interviews with the first cohort to use the fully developed networked learning environment, that it has been used so far in a way that linked to the overall course in a useful way but that the work done within the environment was primarily for assessment purposes plus, to a lesser degree, for preparing for the residential workshops. As they explained;

> One of the main learning activities performed within the online environment relates to the collaborative assessment of assignments. There are discussions on the selection of the topic and focus of assignments, help and advice whilst doing the work and, finally, there is a process of collaborative assessment of assignments, all of which take place within the learning set discussion areas.
>
> (Hodgson and Zenios 2003: 407)

This general picture was confirmed in a second study which focused on where and how learners operated within the networked learning environment (Hodgson and Watland 2004). This study, which looked at where participants visited and what they actually did when using the different areas of the networked learning environment, found that participants tended to focus on what they needed to be doing to complete their assignments for assessment. In some cases they appeared not very concerned about what others were doing for their assignments, as I will discuss in more detail below.

Examination of online set discussions

The primary concern with matters related to doing work for assignments for assessment is frequently reflected in the content of the online set discussions. Knowing that this is the primary use of the networked learning environment offers an opportunity to study the way learners and tutors carry out their discussions about assessment within the learning sets.

In the online discussion it is not unusual to see that what often begins as mostly a discussion about one person's assignment can become, through numerous postings over the course of several days, both a wider and more reflective discussion than when it first started.

For example, one discussion thread started by being essentially focused on what one participant was proposing for his dissertation and how viable or relevant people felt the ideas and thinking to be. Over four to five days the discussion developed into a conversation that moved beyond what was being proposed as a dissertation topic to a wider ranging and meta-level discourse on what are the boundaries of management learning. The level of the online conversations can be quite specific and at a micro-level of detail about, for example, what to read, what to include and how to structure one's work. Equally, it can be a more meta-level discussion related to emergent topics and ideas. In most cases the work required for assessment does pervade the online interactions; however, course participants do appear to be able to carry on conversations without obvious constant recourse to the institutional power and assessment processes that, in a sense, underpin the *raison d'être* for having the conversation at all. The experience of institutional power does nonetheless appear to be an omnipotent presence throughout most learning-set discussions. This is, perhaps, best illustrated in the way participants' comments and responses often tend to be either qualified or modulated in nature.

For example, one participant made the following interesting, but qualified, response to ideas 'Peter' had proposed:

> Peter – this sounds really interesting and I know I'll learn alot!
> Trouble with grounded theory (the little I know about it) is that it must take ages for the theory to emerge – aren't you supposed to start with nothing? That doesn't sound like you! But it could also be a serious time problem. Isn't an enthographic study better? (Now I really am in deep water) but I've started so I'll keep going. i.e. – if you were to identify an element of the study that interests you deeply, you could then research it through an exploration of the perspectives of different stakeholders? Don't know whether this is right or useful …
> I'll stop – as I said, I know I'll learn lots!

On the other hand, comments from tutors frequently appear to reflect feelings of responsibility for managing the disciplinary boundaries of what is acceptable or legitimate knowledge or research to include in an assignment for an MA in Management Learning. For example the tutor comments to Peter:

> Hi Peter – clearly an interesting opportunity for you but I must confess I am wondering where in your description is the management learning angle and whether you are going perhaps too far in the direction of organisational studies? I suppose you would need to think in terms of the learning perspective/theories that might be relevant to the study you end up doing. There is the work that you have to do and there is the dissertation and although they may be situated in the same context I think there needs to be an awareness of how they differ.

Throughout their discussions both learners and tutors appear to be aware that the assessment requirements of the institution have to be respected and are a constraint upon what any of them can offer or do. It is not difficult to identify the presence of the technologies of power of both examination and confession in such a process. Peter, for example, feels obliged to explain to the tutor some of his reasons:

> Maybe I find a way to ease both requirements (Maml and work project). The challenge is that the client and me agreed on a distinct research agenda. My possibilities to circumvent or change it during my research would be dangerous and ethically speaking I would have to get an agreement with the client. I am still not convinced why such a case could not be used for Maml purposes.

However, despite or even because of this, it appeared that participants were still able to engage in discussions that had all the hallmarks of deep learning; take for example the rest of Peter's comment:

> I remember some papers which focused on organisational behaviour stuff and analysed power and gender or decision processes or group dynamics which are mainly topics of social psychology. At this point there were no objections to these choices. I also remember our mapping exercise with Mark (individual, group and organisational learning) that opened up perspectives on phenomenon that are not solely learning-related but broader items of organisation sociology (politics, emotional labour, group think, human resource management, phenomenology of groups, racism ...). We even discussed the images of organisations by Morgan. What is the specific definition of Management Learning? What is in, what is out, where are the boundaries? Let's first sort this out then before I defend my case too strong.

In the many examples of online discussion threads there is little evidence to be found of approaches to learning that could be described as either strategic or surface. We cannot conclude, however, that all participants on the programme engage in the kind of meta-level or deep-learning discussions just described.

Learners' description of their experience

Returning to the experience of some participants interviewed by Hodgson and Watland, they found evidence to suggest some participants' approach might be better described as strategic in their orientation to assessment, as one learner explained:

> Frankly once I have gotten involved in getting into my assignment, I can read someone else's but it is a bit of a passing interest to be honest. What I am really concerned with is I have a couple of other books to read or spend two hours on the library web and I would rather do that then spend a hour going through someone's draft paper and sending them a couple of pages worth of comments on it ... that would not be a constructive use of my time.

What this comment also suggests is that by being strategic in this way learners are likely to pursue more of an individual orientation to learning than is possibly assumed for most learner-centred designs and for participative assessment approaches specifically. This in turn can potentially affect how learners experience the feedback and marking part of the process. This can, as the same learner commented, sometimes be experienced as quite superficial:

> I was pleased that someone had obviously read the paper and commented but I have to say that all the comments that I had back from all my colleagues, apart from X (the tutor), were a bit sort of, well, about punctuation or 'I don't quite understand this phrase'. In other words they weren't critical in the sort of academic sense of 'Does this paper make sense, How well was it structured?' ... [The comments I received were not] the sort of comment I was really looking for. I was looking for something a bit more substantial.

In addition, there was evidence of some learning sets electing to adopt more of a strategic approach to the way they worked together. 'Charles', a participant from another cohort, described how the apparently experienced necessity to focus on assignments and to get tutor feedback led, for him, to less productive set discussions and to an end product or task focus. He believed that most of the sets he had worked in had set ground rules that limited what was legitimate content for discussion:

> Only I suppose because the set, most sets that I have been in have stipulated from the outset, some sort of ground rules that it's not meant to chat around 'Hey how's your day?' 'What's happening in your job?' And 'Oh by the way what are you doing on your assignment?'

I think we said it was a more focused set and the past two sets have been the same. So I feel a bit put upon I suppose if I came into this, that I can't just talk to Adam or Jack or Alice and say 'I've had a bad day, how's it going for you'. I don't feel I can say that after those initial discussions, which I feel is a bit disabling.

From what he says, the consequences of this agreed or imposed restricted discussion process between set members resulted for Charles in the experience of a more mechanistic kind of discussion, as he explained:

I'm transacting my ideas, my structure for my seminar paper and 'I want your comments and thank you for yours and I will feedback to you' that kind of transactional thing. I would like it to be broader then that and that has tempered how I do it.

Whilst this was apparently not his preference he explains he is prepared or willing to go along with it for what was essentially assessment purposes.

It make me feel guilty, which is a completely redundant emotion but one I suppose I have chosen to side with, only because there is an end product and deadline, there is a reason for having this, to discuss our ideas to share, to get feedback from the set tutor.

The emotional side of participative assessment seems to be a significant and perhaps under-recognised part of learners' experience. Asensio et al. (2000) found in their study that engaging in particularly the feedback and marking process of participative assessment is often emotional, anxiety provoking and at times distressing, as the following two extracts from their study illustrate, one based on a face-to-face experience and the other on an online experience:

Face-to-face experience:
'There was a feeling of uncertainty. You feel a part of yourself is being exposed and being assessed, so there is a vulnerability.'

Online experience:
'The whole experience was very emotive, I felt pretty distressed about it.'

Equally, in their role as 'assessors', learners can experience uncertainty about whether they are doing it 'right'. This is reflected in the following extract from an email sent by one participant to her tutor about how she was finding it difficult to mark a piece of work that she considered to be borderline:

I know you operate very democratically Jo, but I have very little experience in marking written work hence me mentioning this before we get together next week. I am feeling the pressure of this process and what is the level of a pass because I haven't been in this position before.

And once the marking process is complete there can be feelings of distress or unhappiness sometimes with the outcomes – one participant, for example, concluding the assessment discussion of her work where she had hoped for a better mark with the following comment:

> Okay guys i am tired ... will stick to our mark ... no problems ... my fault having had no time or the time or space of mind ... let's go with the marks you have suggested ... I can accept that on this occasion I may have deserved the lowest mark of the team, but I feel the gap between my paper and Heidi's isn't any greater than the gap between hers and Joan's and Jack's. I thought the mark was on the paper, not on the feedback on the feedback?? Anyway, I'll stick with whatever you guys decide ...

On conventional programmes such expressions of fear and anxiety, as expressed above, are most generally associated with learners adopting a surface approach to learning. There was no evidence to suggest this to be the case when associated with the learners' experience of participative assessment. Whether it contributes to productive learning energy is perhaps more questionable.

Individual versus collective orientation to participative assessment

It appears that there are two approaches emerging here to participative assessment, one that has a more collective orientation and one that has a more individual orientation. Arguably, it is assumed in the design of learner-centred courses that to include participative assessment will involve learners in the responsibility for assessment of their own work and this in turn will, by implication, involve them in the kind of wide-ranging and reflective discussions suggested in the description of one online set's discussion about one of its members' dissertation topic. This may not always be how learners experience participative assessment. Whether because they adopt a strategic approach to assessment or for other reasons related to completing their own assignments, it appears that some learners do not commit to, or involve themselves in, the kind of critically reflective discussion that it is often assumed will be associated with participative assessment approaches.

There was nothing, however, to suggest from either the learners interviewed or the online discussions examined that learners involved in participative assessment adopt a surface approach to learning. Their experience of assessment practices did nonetheless remain significant and pervasive, and, it has to be said, frequently an emotional one that impacted on everything they did and said. Despite this, it appeared that deep-learning outcomes were much more likely to be associated with participative assessment whether or not they adopted an essentially collective or individual orientation to the process.

Perhaps more worrying for advocates of participative assessment practices is that some learners can and often do adopt a more individual orientation and this in turn can lead to sterile and quite mechanistic 'transactions' that do not fulfil the promise and aspirations associated by many with participative assessment. There are many reasons why this might happen and to understand this more, as indicated by Reynolds and Trehan (2000), greater attention needs to given to the process involved and, I would suggest, to the technologies of power embedded within any assessment process.

Concluding remarks

As mentioned in the introduction, there is increasingly a recognition that assessment practices need to change from the dominant tradition of final examination or setting course work that requires little critical or creative thinking from learners. Such approaches generally reflect assumptions about the nature of knowledge as relatively static and stable and, consequently, easily transferable. Today's learners would be better served by assessment approaches that offer them the opportunity to acquire the skills and understanding that will assist them to operate effectively in a diverse, constantly changing, and information rich, orientated world. There are some interesting developments with respect to assessment practice, in particular those associated with adopting an assessment portfolio approach. I would suggest, however, that not enough attention has been given to the learning potential that could accrue from a greater adoption and use of participative assessment approaches. As demonstrated in this chapter, participative assessment, almost without exception, is associated with deep approaches to learning and, perhaps more importantly, brings the learner directly into the assessment process. While assessment remains the route to a higher degree or qualification it will always be associated with institutional power. This, however, adds to the case for moving towards more participative approaches to assessment as then there is, at least, the potential to acknowledge the institutional and, indeed, other power relations and processes that are inevitably involved in any assessment process and to consider ways to handle this with those who are most directly involved and affected, that is with learners themselves.

Acknowledgments

The work of the following colleagues, Mireia Asensio, Michael Reynolds, Kiran Trehan, Philip Watland and Maria Zenios, contributed enormously to the development of the ideas in this paper.

Chapter 4

Postgraduate research students' learning in higher education

Pam Denicolo

Introduction: the significance of research students

Burgess (1997), in a book entitled *Beyond the First Degree*, noted that the shift from elite to mass higher education since the 1980s had resulted in major debates between researchers, practitioners and policy makers about the purposes and nature of postgraduate education and training. While undergraduate education has retained predominance in policy initiatives and public debate since then, post-graduate education has nevertheless continued to move rapidly from the margins of consideration to a more central focus for development and change in the UK and Europe, both within institutions and at national policy levels.

Although the boundaries between taught and research-based postgraduate courses are becoming increasingly blurred, as demonstrated in this chapter by a consideration of the nexus of research training courses and supervision practice on research student learning, the particular focus on postgraduate research in this chapter emerges from both a theoretical rationale and a personal interest. In order to inoculate the reader to the inevitable prejudices inherent in the subsequent sections, it is important to address the latter first by revealing a little relevant personal history since constructivist theory demonstrates how perspectives are influenced by experience. This professional biography also serves to illustrate the context addressed by the policy reforms described later.

A personal interest

It is a common phenomenon that the mores one experiences in youth, or indeed in the early years of experience as a professional, become considered as the norm, providing a baseline from which one measures the extent and effectiveness of change.

My own doctoral degree was undertaken in the early 1980s in an education research institute (IED, Institute of Educational Development) led by Professor Lewis Elton. A sense of the philosophy that pervaded the Institute at that time can be gleaned by reference to an article published in 1989 by Lewis and my doctoral supervisor, Maureen Pope (Elton and Pope 1989) in which they described and advocated a collegial approach to research student supervision and training. This was my norm. It is only in retrospect, as I later worked in other academic departments and institutions that initially conformed to the more general rubric of the times, that I recognised what an unconventional, innovative and formative experience I had undergone as a member of that research group. In brief, the extensive research training programme in the IED emphasised that effective methodological choice depends on being conversant with the full range of options, their strengths and weaknesses; supervision took the form of a joint endeavour, an evolving partnership in which the student's personal autonomy and responsibility for the research were gradually developed; collegiality was evidenced in formal seminars and informal debate to which students were expected to contribute as peers and were encouraged to argue their case. The ambience was one in which we, students and staff, were all learners engaged together to improve teaching, learning and research across all sectors of education, albeit that each one of us individually had a specific research sub-focus on a particular sector and/or aspect of education.

Later in other professional contexts, firstly as a supervisor and then as a Director of Postgraduate Research and Training, I strove to emulate and then disseminate the good practice I had experienced as a student, despite inhabiting environments in which research training was by tradition focused on the skills necessary to complete a particular research project while supervision consisted mainly of passing on the wisdom of the discipline and suggestions about how to construct a thesis. My colleagues were not Luddites. They had good intentions but many of them clung to the familiar and well-understood traditions of postgraduate research supervision and training while much else around them in the professional arena was subject to change, to which other chapters in this book attest.

A more objective rationale

Statistics demonstrate that, although the number of taught postgraduates is increasing, the proportion of postgraduate to undergraduate students in any university is small (HESA 2001). Nevertheless, commentators have stressed that research students are significant beyond their numerical proportion in defining the university (Becher *et al.* 1994, Noble 1994). Such scholars have been said to internalise the authority of the academy through submitting to intellectual mastery (Bourdieu 1990). Thus research degrees play a pre-eminent role not only in the transmission of academic tradition but, more importantly in the current economic and political climate, in the generation of new knowledge and intellectual capital for the benefit of all.

This latter importance is reflected in the growing impetus to attract research students from the professions and industry by providing a range of doctoral degrees, some of which, e.g. professional doctorates, have a greater taught element than traditional doctoral degrees. This diversification in the range, background and motivations of students participating at this level of education (Weil 1997) has added to the worldwide demand for attention to be paid to content and quality in research student education (Zuber-Skerritt and Ryan 1994). This demand originated from staff and student dissatisfaction with traditional support procedures that were unstructured and inadequately funded and monitored. It gained momentum as governments recognised that graduate students have a strong contribution to make to the economic capital of the nation through their future research either in academia or elsewhere.

These points will be elaborated in the next section but from the above it is clear that much of what was formerly taken for granted about research degrees, even a decade ago, can no longer be assumed to be sacrosanct (Green and Shaw 1999).

Changes in policy and thinking about research degrees and research students' learning

Changes in the student population and the nature of Higher Degrees by Research

Researchers throughout the last decade of the twentieth century had already challenged the traditional stereotype of the full-time, funded, young research student (e.g. Denicolo and Pope 1999, Deem and Brehony 2000) when government policy began to focus on widening participation in university education generally. At the same time universities themselves, through an economic imperative, sought to increase student numbers at all levels within the system, but particularly in the high-fee area of postgraduate research. This has led to the enrolment of more part-time, self- or employer-funded, mature home/ EU research students as well as overseas students. Since inclusion is more than simply the incorporation of people from 'non-traditional' backgrounds into the formal, mainly tacit (Parry 1998, Eraut 2000), protocols of Higher Degrees by Research, this has had implications for the training and support of research students, not least because postgraduate research supervision had previously tended to be a one-to-one, labour-intensive activity while training programmes varied in their scope and depth within and between universities.

Contemporaneously, across the sector, 'practice-based' and 'taught doctorates', in which the practical research element is substantially reduced, have proliferated (Winter et al. 1997, Humphrey and McCarthy 1999). Again, such changes have demanded attention to appropriate forms of teaching, learning and assessment that meet the needs of the students and of those who employ them. Curricula which both incorporate additional discipline subject matter yet do justice to the research element are difficult to balance and the debate continues about the equivalence of these different forms of doctorate (Usher 2002).

At a very practical level these changes in student profiles, numbers and course intentions demand some consideration of the timing of teaching and tutorials as well as the content of courses and the approaches used within them. Further, the intellectual support of research students increasingly needs to demonstrate transparent value for money as the public purse funding a minority of students requires more accountability while private funders, employers and students themselves become more informed and hence selective about where to invest scarce resources.

Accelerating policy-driven change permeating the system

Partially in response to these developments, partially in response to a growing demand from within academia but probably mostly as a response to the needs of industry and the economy (see also Laurillard in this book), there has been a general European trend of government policy-driven changes in the system (Gellert 1993, Denicolo 1998). In the UK the Winfield Enquiry (Winfield 1987) and the Harris Review (Harris 1996) each contributed refinements to plans to transform the purpose, structure and process of Higher Degree by Research studies. Thus by the turn of the century it was clear that it was no longer sufficient for research students to become learned in the specific literature and proficient in the philosophy and methods relevant to their chosen project. They must also be able to demonstrate broader research skills across a range of methodologies and techniques, having been supported both practically and intellectually in their institutions to acquire them.

Institutions themselves became rapidly more alert to the need for internal consistency of provision and for the need to be accountable to outside agencies for their provision. During the 1990s, in a context that included *inter alia* concerns to improve submission rates, to cope with increasing student numbers and diversity yet to acknowledge the essential isolation of research students, most institutions established centralised forms of monitoring progress while several went further and set up one or more Graduate Schools.

In 1999, the Quality Assurance Agency published a code of practice in relation to quality and standards in postgraduate research degrees while Funding Councils produced exacting standards for research training to be met by institutions seeking recognition for their courses for funding purposes. Research too had become increasingly directed towards the doctorate, providing evidence to the policy makers: completion rates, student selection, research training programmes and supervision procedures all received attention (e.g. Hockey 1994, Black *et al.* 1994, Burgess 1996, Acker 1999), with anomalies, disparities and areas of neglect being increasingly made explicit. In the conferences of learned societies such as the Society for Research in Higher Education (SRHE) and the UK Council for Graduate Education (UKCGE), academics produced papers and discussed at an unprecedented level their experiences in the fields of, for instance, supervision and research degree examining (e.g. Delamont *et al.* 2000, Tinkler and Jackson 2000, Hartley and Fox 2002, Denicolo 2003, Denicolo in press). As regret was overtly being expressed at both the grass-roots level and at policy level about these issues, it seemed as if a veil had been lifted and that the time was ripe for more radical initiatives.

These soon appeared; indeed they proliferated. In 2002, a report to the Higher Education Funding Councils for England, Scotland and Wales, entitled *Improving*

Standards in Postgraduate Research Degree Programmes (Metcalfe *et al.* 2002), was distributed to all UK higher education institutions. This took the form of a consultative document to review good practice, determine the role of threshold standards and identify indicators that could be used to monitor attainment of threshold standards. Institutions were alerted that funding was to become conditional on achieving these minimum standards. Building on responses, a further consultation document was published in May 2003 which contained revisions that attempted to address concerns expressed by the community about: numerical targets, which did not recognise the different training requirements of separate disciplines or would be difficult to achieve in small units; the little regard paid to the requirements of part-time, mature or overseas students; the explicit but inappropriate link between a unit's Research Assessment grade and the quality of the postgraduate research support provided.

The implications of the final policy directive have been linked with those contained in: the White Paper entitled *The Future of Higher Education* (DfES 2003a); the Roberts Report *Set for Success* (Roberts 2003); and a communication from the Commission of the European Communities to the Council and European Parliament entitled *Researchers in the European Research Area: One Profession, Multiple Careers* (2003). Each of these documents emphasised the need to change the way graduate students are prepared for research, suggesting that more attention be paid to enhancing employability through training in core research skills and wider employment related skills. In addition to proposing that training aspects will need to be strengthened considerably across the sector, and that funding will be dependent on achieving this, each document acknowledged the central importance of high quality supervision.

Impact on learning and teaching

The impact of this accelerating change in how research degree studies are interpreted impacts directly on three groups of people: the students, their supervisors and those who design and deliver training programmes. The changes to development/training programmes for both students and staff will be addressed first, followed by a consideration of their reactions to the process and its outcomes.

Developments in training and support

At different rates over the last 15 years, institutions have been revising their provision for research student support in response to the conditions described above. There has been an increasing shift away from small-scale, individual research training of students by the supervisor towards larger-scale course provision at school/department, faculty and even institution level. By the 1990s most students could expect to benefit from training in the basic research skills of their discipline in the company of their peers, at least for their first year, and the breadth of that training was beginning to increase in response to the demands of the Funding Councils.

As mentioned previously, in some institutions Graduate Schools were established, though they adopted different models: some were institution-wide organisations; others were restricted to particular faculties within an institution. Although the aim of all was to improve graduate education, some had a predominantly administrative/monitoring remit while others focused more on academic programmes (UKCGE 1995). Whatever the model, the formal taught component was again generally 'layered', with some classes on generic topics for a large group of students, discipline-specific topics addressed in smaller groups and supervisors taking responsibility to tailor learning to the specific projects of their students.

Although the driving force may have been to teach a wider range and depth of topics more efficiently, at the level of the students' experience there were other potential advantages to this change in provision. Opportunities came into being for engagement with a broader range of philosophies and methods and with a larger number of subject experts. Further, the solitariness of doctoral research was beginning to be ameliorated as students at least sat in class with their peers, though the needs of part-time students were seldom considered. However, despite a general encouragement across the sector to present sessions in a more student-centred, interactive mode (in the style of constructivist approaches as described in this book by Boud), it seems that this has yet to pervade all postgraduate research training, even in disciplines in which it might most be expected such as education.

In a recent residential workshop, funded by the ESRC and the British Educational Research Association (BERA), a sadly large number of participants from institutions across the UK reported little previous opportunity to debate issues with either their peers or academic experts (compare this with McConnell's description in Chapter 7 of learning as a way of being in the social world and Laurillard's encouragement in Chapter 6 of working within a community of practice). Some were surprised at how willing to help and approachable the expert presenters at the workshop were. Their previous experience had been of the traditional didactic pedagogy in which they were expected to imbibe the received wisdom imparted by aloof professors. In counterpoint, the presenters, also drawn from dispersed institutions, spoke of their enjoyment of the engagement of these students in debates, of the stimulation the students provided by their incisive questions and so on, reflecting as they expressed this on the pressures of time and conflicting duties that marked their usual interaction with students. This highlights the crux of the matter. There appears to be no lack of willingness to improve the educational experience of postgraduate research students but academics frequently lack the time in a dense programme either to implement appropriate teaching/learning techniques or to develop them because of the escalating demands of administration and for research productivity.

It is not only in the realm of the research training programme per se that there is a need for the further training of staff because supervisors have themselves been a 'neglected species' (Knowles 1978). The training and support of supervisors has historically been disregarded (Elton and Pope 1989) with a few notable exceptions (e.g. Delamont *et al.* 2000, Holbrook and Johnston 1999, Zuber-Skerritt and Ryan 1994). The assumption was that the possession of a research degree or equivalent research experience should prove adequate preparation for the task of supervising others in the field. The prevailing model, for new researchers/students and for new supervisors, was that of apprenticeship in which it was assumed that skills of inducting a novice into the mysteries of the craft could be learnt, mainly from a sole supervisor in the case of students and a mentor in the case of supervisors, through a traditional 'transmission of knowledge' approach. Experienced supervisors, however, recognise their remit as a complex, demanding task, fraught with hurdles (Clegg and Gall 1998, Denicolo *et al.* 1999, Denicolo and Pope 1999) so that the apprentice model can no longer be considered adequate. While qualifications and/or experience of research are necessary conditions for good supervision, they are no longer sufficient.

Since the Harris Report (1996), institutions have been developing mechanisms for supporting and developing their research awards supervisors. Just as in the training of research students, a number of models have developed from institution-wide approaches to provision at faculty, school or departmental level. The provision may be relatively informal and unstructured or formal and accredited. The BBSRC (Biotechnology and Biological Sciences Research Council) has taken a lead through the Training and Accreditation Programme for Postgraduate Supervisors (TAPPS) (Cryer and Mertens 2002). While there have been reports published of individual initiatives, no studies to date have attempted to evaluate the relative success of the various models.

The educational philosophies underpinning these developments in supervisor training are eclectic while it appears that few of the programmes in operation are based on the teaching/learning theories that inform other realms of education practice (MacDonald and Wisdom 2002). However, a considerable literature exists on the continuing professional development of lecturers/teachers (for example, Van Manen 1991, Cowan 1998, Clegg *et al.* 2002) in which reflective practice is advocated. In turn, this is supported by a body of research that demonstrates appropriate means of developing the required skills and advocates support mechanisms to achieve this (Schön 1983, Schön 1987, Mezirow 1990, Clandinin and Connelly 2000). It is both concerning and sad that the theory and practice long established in teacher training departments in higher education have taken so long to percolate through its own system. For example, Schwartz (2004) argued that it is time that psychology took heed of its own research, as other disciplines are beginning to do, by introducing active and problem-based learning (see Boud's chapter again) to undergraduate students. In this book, however, Stefani notes that it is difficult to encourage experienced staff to continuously reflect on and develop their approaches to teaching.

This same literature and research, including that concerned with experiential learning, would also inform the practice of those aiming to produce research training courses for graduate students. It would be valuable too to the students themselves who are expected to compile, through self-directed learning, personal/professional development profiles (PDPs) or portfolios that demonstrate their learning of generic, transferable research skills.

These PDPs, based on Training Needs Analysis, were included in a potential strategy framework, based on the policies proposed in the documents cited in the previous section, commended to universities by Cameron (2004), Chairman of the Research Councils UK Postgraduate Training Group. In order that students have support for their development needs, there is a requirement that institutions provide them with training in employment-related skills (e.g. research management, communication and negotiation skills, intellectual property rights, networking and team-working). Such training is described in the documents as an additional two weeks per year of registration to the current research training provision while the topics to be included in the training are those identified in the UK and European documents as skill areas that employers are currently finding lacking in PhD graduates. It is suggested that too much emphasis has been placed on preparing researchers for an academic research setting, with a veiled implication that this promotes autonomy but neglects collaborative enterprise (remnants of the old image of the lone scientist working in an ivory tower).

This raises a further link between the training needs of students and of supervisors. All the recent documents previously cited include a recommendation that, instead of sole supervision arrangements, students should in future be supported by supervisory teams or committees. This is in acknowledgement not just of the increasingly multi- or inter-disciplinary nature of new research projects but also of the problems caused when a supervisor becomes ill/leaves employment, or when the student–supervisor relationship otherwise becomes unsatisfactory. Although most institutions now have a policy that novice supervisors should work with an experienced colleague till they gain their first successful completion, few academics have experience of supervising together in a larger group and may need to develop both strategies and skills for doing so. As was noted in the 2003 White Paper (DfES 2003a), all of these changes to postgraduate research training and support constitute a radical shift from traditional practice and attitudes.

Living and working with these developments

The first thing to be raised in this section is the language of the documents. Colleagues who count among the enthusiasts for radical transformation in postgraduate research teaching and learning regret that the vocabulary permeating all the recent policy documents has the potential to act as a barrier to implementation, since it derives from industry. My description of the policy changes reflects that terminology in seeking to convey the tenor of those documents. Some examples from the documents will further illustrate this: 'profiting' from postgraduate talent; 'investing' in research; the academic 'market'; 'training needs analysis' and so on. More conducive language is needed if we are to avoid alienating colleagues when disseminating these ideas and policies.

Other barriers to change also exist, as evidenced by the slow and patchy adoption across the sector of policy directives. One of the major stumbling blocks has been alluded to earlier, that is the continuous and unrelenting additions to the roles and remits of academics: at the undergraduate and taught Masters' level and now at the postgraduate research level.

Two other common concerns have been expressed frequently by colleagues across the sector. One focuses on equity of support and training provision for all students registered for Higher Degrees by Research. The current policies provide additional funding for Research Council funded students only, who usually represent only a small proportion of all research students within an institution. There is, however, a general expectation that means will be found to provide such learning opportunities to all students. In plenary discussions with representatives of the Funding Councils (UK Grad Programme 2004), suggestions were made about raising further financial support for the courses using the leverage principle to encourage other funders, charities and employers, for instance, to contribute higher fees. Although these possibilities are likely to be considered, they will take time to implement while in the meantime courses need to be planned and run. In addition, this possible course of action ignores the self-funded students and neglects consideration of the ramifications of raising overseas fees in an environment of global competition.

Colleagues' second main concern is that the students will be distracted from the substance of their projects by the numerous other expectations imposed on them. Projections are made that the quality of projects will diminish or registration periods may need to be extended to accommodate the extra learning opportunities, with serious implications for the departments' completion rates. Further disquiet arises about the range of expertise available within small units to service the courses. Although colleagues hear the rhetoric that minimum standards can be achieved through cooperation between departments or institutions, there is an understandable resistance to the dilution of their autonomy, especially as their potential partners may be competitors for students or in the research field. Some view this as somewhat akin to collaboration with the enemy, similar to Ashwell's (2003) finding about multi-professional teams in the health and social services. Equally, resistance to change may come from experienced professionals objecting to being 'de-skilled' and thus requiring 'training'. Those who have seen many doctoral students through to successful completion using 'tried and tested' approaches and methods may see little point in the imposed change unless they are more assiduously engaged by a convincing theoretical argument as opposed to an economic one.

Students too need to be informed and convinced. Although many of them welcome styles of teaching and learning that recognise them as competent adults with much to contribute as well as learn, it is not yet clear that these styles will be incorporated into new courses in the rush, with limited resources, to provide programmes that comply with government imperatives. Further, students are not a homogeneous group. Amongst other things they pursue research degrees to meet different purposes while their varied prior experience of higher education predisposes them towards different learning approaches. For instance, some undoubtedly embark on their new studies eager to take advantage of every learning opportunity provided while others perceive a research degree as an opportunity to devote their attention to a burning research issue in their chosen field or profession. Depending on the culture in which their prior higher education learning took place, students are differentially prepared for the self-directed learning described as the foundation for the development of PDPs. In the past, individual supervision provided a means for the gradual development of research independence from the individual student's starting point and at his/her own pace. This could prove difficult to incorporate into a timetable of generic and specialised courses and with a larger team of supervisors.

This section has addressed only some of the issues raised for participants by recent changes in policy and thinking about the learning of postgraduate research students; more will certainly emerge as policy is translated into practice.

The future: what might and ought to be

These are certainly 'interesting times' in the sense of the Chinese benediction. Twenty years ago the loud cries of the few stalwarts devoted to trying to improve the learning/support of postgraduate research students and their supervisors seemed to fall on deaf ears within and without the academy. Suddenly, it seems, external powers have caught some of the echoes, at least those that resonate with current economic imperatives, with the result that this once neglected sector has become the focus for radical change.

How beneficial this change will be for student learning depends greatly on how it is implemented. Along with many colleagues intimately involved in developing and providing support for this group of students, I welcomed the first indications that their needs were at last being considered and efforts were being made through codes of practice etc. to improve student support. The introduction of minimum standards of training and support seemed another step in the right direction. Nevertheless it seems that the apocryphal stories of the research student abandoned to produce a thesis with only irregular and infrequent supervisory support might be relegated to the past. Instead, for some academics, a different spectre arises – the 'mass produced' researcher, trained through a series of pre-ordained courses or 'hoops' to perform research tasks that serve the economy ... perhaps this is another example of the bittersweet flavour of success that Boud refers to in his chapter.

This is a worst-case scenario, just as the abandoned student represents isolated cases or an extreme example. Careful reading of the text of the cited documents reveals laudable intentions: that students will draw on their training opportunities to further their personal and professional development, that they be supported to become flexible, 'well-rounded' researchers able to adapt skills through knowledge to meet ever changing research problems and circumstances.

To achieve those aims requires more than the mere provision of courses that demonstrate compliance and secure future funding. Instead, careful consideration needs to be given to a plethora of interrelated matters. In a roughly ascending order of specificity, these are: how to create a sustainable and integrated approach to research student support within institutions; how to transform change into development, building on what is already good in the system rather than replacing it; how to convey the worth of the useful ideas contained within policy documents to current and future staff and students; how to integrate skills learning with research education and research practice, through the development of active/experiential teaching and learning strategies; how to adapt internal and nationally agreed procedures to allow appropriate time both for the supervision process and the development of supervisory skills, and indeed to provide incentive to supervisors to engage in these activities.

Careful consideration too must be given to the, as yet relatively unexplored, ramifications of increasing the amount and breadth of learning engaged in by research students. One of these is the amount of time necessary to achieve this additional learning alongside completing a research project intended to demonstrate an original contribution to knowledge. Submission rates have been a considerable focus of attention in order to reduce them in recent years – some revision of this ideal may well be required. In parallel with this the assessment criteria for the award of the PhD could bear some attention. Recent literature (Denicolo 2003, Murray 2003) has included discussion of the vagueness of published criteria and the diversity of what aspects are addressed, and with what weighting, in UK universities. Certainly the advent of the new training initiatives, added to the proliferation of different kinds of doctorate, demands a detailed and informed debate across the sector about what constitutes 'doctorateness', especially to allay concerns about critical thinking becoming secondary to more practical skills.

In conclusion, the changes in prospect amplify the provision that I took for granted as a doctoral student and radically extend that which I later found to be a more general norm. My initial relief that attention was at last being paid to this particular group of students and academics has been tempered, though, by a fear that institutions will be propelled for funding reasons into action that consists of laying new courses, hastily devised, as a veneer on established practice. It will take a concerted effort, through the measured addressing of all the implications and ramifications by those charged with developing and providing postgraduate research training and support across the sector, to ensure that policy is translated into workable, productive practice. We could well heed the advice of the Romans: *carpe diem* but *festina lente*; seize the opportunity but make haste slowly.

Chapter 5

Non-traditional learners in higher education

Will Bridge

Introduction

Like many of the contributors to this book, I started my higher education career graduating from a traditional undergraduate degree, the 'delivery' of which I felt left considerable room for research, development and improvement. As a doctoral student, my postgraduate studies with Lewis Elton took me first into the realms of non-traditional university teaching methodologies (Boud *et al.* 1975), and then on into the study of non-traditional learners in higher education. The latter area has held a fascination for me for the past 30 years.

This chapter explores the wide range of changes which have affected non-traditional learners in higher education since the 1970s. It also identifies some areas where change has been slow or even thwarted. For example, non-traditional student numbers have not expanded as much as they could or should, nor has their socio-economic and ethnic background diversified until recently. Their disciplinary focus, and indeed their basic motivation, has changed significantly – towards the vocational and career-orientated, although liberal adult higher education remains healthy in some areas. And whilst some non-traditional students (most of whom have outside commitments far greater than the conventional 18- to 21-year-old undergraduate) have been liberated from the long-recognised shortcomings of learning through lectures (Bligh 1971), substituting open or distance learning for time serving on campus, this has only been achieved through a series of expansive but flawed initiatives (Duke 1997).

In the 1970s, UK and indeed world university teaching practice was dominated by three-year programmes for full-time undergraduates. They accounted for 90 per cent of the 600,000 student population of the UK's higher education sector in 1970/71 (DfES/HESA data quoted in Jobbins 2003). For the purpose of this chapter, I will regard most of these undergraduates, plus full-timers on taught and research postgraduate degrees, and those on full-time Higher National Diplomas (HNDs) and latterly full-time Foundation Degrees, as the university sector's 'traditional' learners.

The remaining 'non-traditional' students, almost all of whom were undertaking courses that were either short-term or part-time, or both, were a very varied group comprising:

- Part-time postgraduate, first degree and sub-degree students;
- Students studying extra-mural and external degrees – again largely part-time;
- Adult students undertaking professional updating courses linked to their field of employment, or aiming to retrain into new fields of work, or to prepare them for what was then the impending avalanche of occupational change, particularly what we now know as the 'IT revolution';
- Students studying at a distance, by correspondence or through the earliest manifestations of educational technology such as programmed learning.

Thus for the purposes of this chapter, I am primarily focusing upon students studying via non-traditional course modes, delivery methods and qualifications, whilst recognising that other 'non-traditional' aspects of university participation have also emerged over 30 years. One of these involves changes in the student population itself, and the gradual emergence of a more diverse range of students within our traditional course portfolio.

In this second area of non-traditional student backgrounds, there have been three main trends: the growth of overseas students; the 'maturing' age of the university population; and, with increasing higher education participation rates, growing numbers of students whose family and socio-economic background would not have traditionally led them to university.

The just-discernable profile of these non-traditional courses and non-traditional students in the university world of the 1970s started to increase at about the same time as the emergence of a new breed of university academics, variously describing themselves 'educational technologists' such as Elton (1973), and 'educational developers' such as Clark (1981).

From the outset, these early higher education activists found many areas for cross-fertilisation between learning and teaching methods developed for traditional and non-traditional courses and students (Duke 1997). Indeed, much of the early stimulus for educational technology progress in higher education came from non-traditional sources. Examples included the need to update staff working in high technology firms (such as Xerox) in emerging technologies by means of off-campus distance-learning approaches, some of which employed the earliest manifestations of computer-based learning. Thus, as I will illustrate throughout this chapter, the growth of non-traditional higher education teaching methods and that of non-traditional students has become closely linked, with some of the resulting innovations then being transferred for use by conventional courses and students.

Overall trends

Over the 30 years between 1972 and 2002, the total number of students in higher education increased enormously around the world – in the UK the growth was from 0.6 to 1.9 million. Most of this growth came in traditional full-time home undergraduate student expansion between the late 1980s and late 1990s. During this period the number of first-year full-time undergraduates grew from 220,000 to 650,000, many of whom were attending the universities which were newly created in 1992 (HESA data in Jobbins 2003 and Dugdale 1997).

Non-traditional learners in the largest category – that of part-time higher education students in British universities – have contributed far less to this numbers boom, both in the UK and the OECD group of nations (OECD 2003). The one exception is that of taught part-time postgraduate numbers, whose volume has actually grown fastest in percentage terms, albeit from a low 50,000 base in the 1970s, to 250,000 now.

Part-time first degree student numbers barely changed from 1972 to 1992. Their volume dipped significantly in the mid-1990s before resuming the slow upward path they are currently on. This still leaves UK higher education with only 120,000 part-time first degree students and 370,000 'other undergraduate' part-time students in 2002/3 – about 20 per cent (by head count, and of course, far less by full-time equivalent) of the total university population.

The above statistics might be taken as suggesting that the development, and the impact, of non-traditional learners in universities is relatively unimportant compared with the full-time undergraduate steamroller. This would be quite wrong. Whilst previous DfES and the HESA data is reasonably robust on trends in some areas of non-traditional student volume (such as part-time undergraduate numbers), there is evidence, for example that which can be accessed through universities' financial accounts, of significant commercial and short course income growth (Creagh and Graves 2003). With this must have come expansion of non-traditional course volumes and student numbers, some of which have not been captured in national statistics. This should also be seen alongside the HESA 'other undergraduate part-time' category, which did show a rapid increase from 110,000 in 1994 to 370,000 in 2001.

The growing cohort of non-traditional students within UK universities' recent overall expansion record is also important because, in practice, the boundaries between full-time and part-time higher education are reducing, and may be lost altogether in the future. For example, it is now clear that few current full-time undergraduates progress through their three-year programmes without undertaking some level of part-time employment (Fazackerley 2004). A further, less quantifiable trend is for these traditional full-timers to conduct their studies increasingly independently. Reports of traditional undergraduates 'taking away' from the university environment course material and really extensive curriculum components (such as major IT-based assignments), to work on from well-resourced home computer facilities, are now widespread, and the subject of consultations about future national strategies (DfES 2003b). Indeed, this trend has already started to impact upon, for example, our universities' building programmes, library/learning resources, and course delivery plans. This blurring of the traditional/non-traditional student boundary is the start of a significant challenge to university planning which in turn will affect academic staffing, premises, and learning resource issues in future, and further illustrates the profound effect which non-traditional students are having on our universities.

Changes in policy, thinking and the practice of higher education for non-traditional learners

Policy

UK government policy – pursued with varied conviction over the past 30 years – has been to promote the expansion of non-traditional learners in universities. This has largely been as a result of pressure from industrialists and economists, who, as early as the 1980s, were influential in gearing programmes by the Manpower Services Commission (the forerunner of the Learning and Skills Council for England (LSC)) towards vocational higher education. Their ongoing message has been the economically significant role which professional and vocational education, delivered to mature and mid-career students via non-traditional routes, has been found to have in the UK, Europe and worldwide (Burgess 1997). Thus policy initiatives like the Professional, Industrial and Commercial Updating programme in the 1980s, the Open Tec programme of the same era, and a series of policy incentives and exhortations since then (Creagh and Graves 2003) have all been applied to the university sector.

The position of educational technology and university teaching practice developments in these non-traditional higher education student policy initiatives has been variable (Hodgson *et al.* 1987). The Open University (OU) might be regarded as the first and still the most significant concentration of non-traditional learners in UK higher education. The OU's progressive educational development stance, its dependence upon distance-learning materials, and its track record of intelligently harnessing each new generation of ICT delivery vehicles stands out as a significant exception of a rather depressing rule of other short-term UK policy initiatives in open learning for non-traditional students, including various 'Open Colleges' (Watson and Bowden 2002). With a few honourable exceptions, these have failed to produce significant expansion in non-traditional provision, or affect the fundamental focus of UK universities and the mainstream activities upon which they have been grafted.

The complexion of UK politics has of course changed substantially over the past 30 years. However, support policies for non-traditional learners in higher education did not change with the incoming Labour government, nor did the impact of its initiatives in this area improve significantly. New schemes such as the 'University for Industry', the 'e-University' and the government's encouragement of 'corporate universities', all of which emphasise non-traditional learners and non-traditional teaching methods, are just the latest evidence of this disconnected policy area. So far, these have produced modest results compared with both the OU and the steady growth of non-traditional student provision by 'conventional' universities.

Almost all the UK's higher education policy developments in this area have been focused upon the growth of vocational non-traditional higher education. This is notwithstanding the continued success of some forms of liberal adult part-time higher education, as delivered by specialist providers such as Birkbeck College within London University, and the Open University's widespread programme in the arts, humanities, social sciences, and more general adult education.

One industry trend has resulted in particularly tangible growth in non-traditional learners in UK higher education. This is exemplified by the rapid expansion of the part-time MBA as a key plank of many current universities' part-time portfolio. Business/management part-time postgraduate education has grown at a more rapid rate over the past 30 years than any other postgraduate subject area, using a mixture of traditional and non-traditional learning methods. Part-time MBAs address the changing context of UK and world employment, and reflect a wide range of cognitive and affective targets. Corresponding teaching methods for the typically mature and often critical and outspoken non-traditional students of such management programmes have drawn liberally upon developments in educational technology in some, if not all, the universities where significant part-time MBA growth has been seen (QAA 2001).

Over the last 30 years, government policy towards universities in the UK and indeed worldwide has of course identified a number of priorities beyond that of simply growing student numbers. The future of non-traditional students and learning/teaching approaches was a key element of the landmark Dearing Report (NCIHE 1997a). A key associated thrust has been to expand 'third leg' commercial income streams, alongside universities' traditional teaching and research revenue 'legs' (Creagh and Graves 2003 chart this trend in both the UK and Australia).

A further and more recent policy trend has been pressure for university (and indeed further education college and secondary school) specialisation. This is often linked to collaborations between successful institutions, and mergers between those which lack critical mass, or are struggling with the big business of today's higher education environment. Both these policies have had an effect on non-traditional learners. For example, specialisation has helped those with clear vocational goals to select appropriate universities. Collaborations and mergers may also maintain the benefits of scale which permit non-vocational curriculum areas to remain on offer to, for example, part-time students.

Recently, government policy has identified, highlighted and promoted two of the three 'non-traditional students on traditional course' groups referred to in the introduction. These are international students, and students from non-traditional socio-economic and educational backgrounds.

The latter group have usually been defined by one of a range of pretty crude measures, including: geography, i.e. students who find their way to university from neighbourhoods where higher education participation is rare; demography, i.e. those from a family background devoid of university or college experience; or prior achievement, particularly applicants with weaker levels of school-level attainment. A decade of UK-wide initiatives aiming to 'widen opportunity' to these groups has earmarked extra funding streams for universities recruiting and retaining such students. This in turn has made a contribution to the learning process and particular study support provision in higher education institutions which have at least taken this seriously as a new funding stream. The incentives to widen participation of non-traditional students on traditional undergraduate courses have prompted valuable research, development and implementation of initiatives in areas such as: pre-undergraduate programme diagnostic testing and individualised remedial provision; study support and guidance programmes, including (at last) effective recognition and response to special needs such as dyslexia; and the growth of APEL – the assessment of prior and experiential learning (Evans 2001). Here again we see evidence of the impact which non-traditional learners are having on teaching and learning for the whole university population.

Whilst government policy on widening participation has had the above clearly positive effects upon higher education processes, its effectiveness in expanding the number of students from non-traditional socio-economic backgrounds progressing into universities has been harder to identify. This is an area in which longitudinal data is limited and unreliable, but case studies (such as Forsyth and Furlong 2002) are beginning to build up a picture of at least pockets of growth.

International students are the most recent group of non-traditional students to become the focus of government policy. Indeed, until the mid-1990s the efforts of just a handful of UK universities, often working closely with the British Council, were the sum total of concerted UK effort in this field (Donaldson 1994), as North American and Australian universities rapidly developed effective means of 'targeting' these non-traditional learners. Now the focus of both individual university and government recruitment drives, international students' increasing impact upon the UK universities they attend is referred to below.

Changes in thinking about non-traditional learners in higher education

Perhaps the most important 'thinking change' relates to the importance of non-traditional learning within the world of employment. Here, the past 30 years have seen an acceptance in many fields that a full-time first degree, undertaken at the start of a career, is not enough higher education to last a lifetime. The IT revolution, increased professionalism and global competition affecting the workplace, new specialisms in many occupations, and the changing nature of employment and the economy have all reinforced this change of thinking. As a result, far more people now become non-traditional learners attached (sometimes quite loosely) to universities than was the case in the early 1970s. This is true whether they are 'sent' on an MBA by a benevolent employer; or supported through a health and safety management programme by a trade union; or prompted by a period of unemployment to return to university for, say, IT skills updating.

As businesses have become more knowledge-based, sending employees back to become non-traditional university students has been an obvious expedient. However, it is one which firms have resisted taking where the higher education learning and teaching methods on offer are perceived as overly traditional or otherwise 'inefficient'. This is particularly true in the case of ICT-oriented non-traditional higher education, where employers have been outspoken in their requirements for up-to-date teaching equipment and teaching technologies (LSC 2002).

Universities which have catered for this demand have found such non-traditional students to be amongst their most critical of 'customers', and particularly intolerant of mediocre higher education teaching practices (Duke 1997). Nevertheless, non-traditional learners on vocational updating courses tend to be amongst the most committed of all to pursuing the objective-based approaches to learning and teaching which were first promoted in the educational technology approaches for which Elton (1999) remains a key advocate. They have also become decreasingly inclined to value the 'time-serving' or social group justifications for conventional delivery methods, particularly where these involve ill-prepared lectures or aimless practical work.

Overall my thinking is that the pressures of increased managerialism in the world of employment, linked to the impact of digital technology in the workplace, have combined to create a pattern of threats and opportunities which have strongly encouraged non-traditional student growth in the form of employees in mid-career – a trend which will both prompt specialisation and development of provision. These pressures have also given those who participate successfully a real sense of being 'ahead of the pack', having benefited from a personal stake in what is recognised as the increasingly financial investment aspect of higher education.

Changes in the practice of non-traditional higher education

As well as policy changes, the practice of non-traditional higher education has also changed markedly over the past 30 years, most fundamentally in terms of where it is located and what it comprises. Extra-mural departments as the key focus for non-traditional practice have given way to participation by most university faculties in non-traditional student programmes. The nature of these programmes varies considerably – from pockets of online and distance learning, through part-time versions of current degree programmes, to recently designed Foundation Degrees, whether full-time or part-time, delivered jointly between universities, further education colleges and sponsoring industries or commercial organisations. There also remain a clutch of specialist entirely non-traditional higher education providers, with OU by far the largest in the sector. Key elements of UK employment are also being targeted by recently pump-primed non-traditional higher education initiatives, aiming to bring supposedly university-level education to industry and commerce (the University for Industry), to the health professions (through the NHSU), and to the world of online undergraduate programmes through the E-University (DfES 2003b).

In most of the UK's recent attempts to expand non-traditional higher education student volumes, a growing assumption tends to be that the resulting practice will be based upon e-learning techniques. This has generated some promising innovations, some inspiring practice, but also a sense of déjà vu in terms of failed impact. Positive examples include the links between the courseware produced for conventional students by higher education institutions, and materials drawn down from the internet by non-traditional learners (see Sklar and Pollack (2000) for a framework of such developments). The resulting applications include practical work animations which are more instructive and accessible than the former requirement for heavy equipment-based workshop, studio or laboratory exercises (Hannan and Silver 2002). There is continuing scope for developments in this field, for example using mobile communication and 'texting' to enhance communication between non-conventional students and their tutors. Indeed, in her IT-orientated chapter in this book, Diana Laurillard foresees 3G mobile communication producing another period of revolution in educational technology.

Overall, the delivery of non-traditional higher education in the workplace seems certain to increase, and with it, links between particular universities and the personnel (and possibly labour organisations) in major industries. University teaching practice will need to adapt to this new positioning and location, and to the increasingly mature non-traditional learners who themselves are part of our 'greying' society.

Analysis and forward look

Teaching and learning methods for non-traditional learners in higher education have come a long way in 30 years. Initially, short courses and updating programmes provided by universities were seen as the opportunity for virtuoso teaching and demonstration performances by particularly up-to-date academics. One widespread example was, and continues to be, the provision of masterclasses as part of short commercial course offers. The future of these non-traditional elements of higher education is closely bound up with the future role of universities in society and the world of work. Increasingly, we see this cutting-edge updating provision translated into the development of learning packs and negotiated consultancy delivered by university staff 'out in industry'.

Overseas students will play an increasingly significant part in both traditional and non-traditional university courses (Scott 1998). Indeed, the globalisation of English as the language of world business and education may produce university courses in which the English language training component – both conversational and profession-specific – is equally valued alongside the academic course content. Notwithstanding the amenability of such hybrid courses to non-traditional teaching methods, such as today's successors of educational technology-based language laboratories, or online tutoring, this expansion of non-traditional overseas student numbers will have fairly conservative effects upon teaching methods and styles – reflecting the tastes and values of many of the participating overseas students.

One complication faced by all spheres of higher education, which will be increasingly well tackled in non-traditional fields, is that of differential course pre-knowledge, and the need for thorough initial diagnostics of students as they commence their courses (Duke 1997). ICT-based pre-tests and profiling, and the systematic assessment of prior and experiential learning will become particularly fundamental to tackling this aspect of higher education of non-traditional learners. However, non-traditional learners will increasingly challenge higher education staff in new ways, not only in terms of their technical expertise and grasp of the current world of work, but also in terms of their learning technology skills, and their ability to liaise with and merge the skills of ICT, learning resources, and information/content experts.

Governments' and universities' thinking must surely change on the value of pump priming further up-front investments in open/distance and e-learning technology courseware. These have been epitomised by past initiatives which have assumed that, to thrive, all that is required is a substantial set-up investment and a high-profile marketing launch. Regularly tested, these assumptions have been found wanting every time.

A further significant trend will be for non-traditional higher education provision to become further commercialised. For example, dual certification of ICT-based non-traditional courses (shared, say, with equipment manufacturers or software houses) will grow rapidly. This may involve overt endorsement and 'licences to practice' or to use particular procedures as widespread as those relating to health and safety, to legal processes, or to new medical techniques. These will bring into the non-traditional university arena a second, closely career-orientated, source of reward for non-traditional learners – above and beyond the simple goal of securing a higher education award.

Notwithstanding the above, it is also predicable that non-traditional courses will move further into the mainstream of higher education, and become less distinctive. This will occur as conventional undergraduate programmes increasingly go online, part-time, and as a result become more attractive to a mature audience selected primarily on their ability to pay, within the new 'top-up' fee environment of the future.

Already the subject of significant international competition, higher education for non-traditional learners will become the most globalised of all arenas of university operation. Indeed, as education and communication technology makes non-traditional higher education decreasingly campus-specific, it will be possible for major international university brands (such as MIT or INSEAD) to compete on technical expertise, courseware investment, and even closeness to fit to individual non-traditional learners' needs the world over.

One relatively unexplored area of non-traditional higher education is the impact which its participants can have on the structure and content of university provision, through the input of their life experience, and their employment expertise. Future programmes for non-traditional learners may therefore contain a more explicit 'knowledge dialogue' element between these students and their academic mentors. Indeed, we may see ICT used expressly to gather participants' experience, and assimilate it into future generations of teaching material. This could result in education technology products with artificial intelligence embedded into their programming and structuring – in areas ranging from simulation and games technology to legal practice. This is a parallel with techniques for evolving teaching/learning procedures and evaluation methods which have been explored for some time (e.g. Themessl-Hubber and Grutsch 2003).

As several observers have commented (for example, Laurillard, quoted earlier), it is also likely that the non-traditional learner of the future will seek higher education teaching methods which are more mobile than is currently the case. Already the requirement is that much of the didactic content of non-traditional higher education should be deliverable online – say through conventional laptop computers and wireless networks. This will be further refined as new generations of mobile communication provide opportunities for delivery of, and more importantly interaction with, intelligent content.

In a similar vein, future non-traditional university programmes will place more emphasis upon their design and imagery. This may result in the long-predicted fusion of education and entertainment – 'edutainment' – and further blurring of the adult liberal education/professional updating boundaries. This should be linked to a more adaptive form of non-traditional education programme for learners – 30 years after Elton complained of the lack of individualisation for conventional full-time undergraduates (Elton *et al.* 1973). Adaptability will be needed in order to respond to the significant differences which a globalised multilingual audience for non-traditional higher education courses will inevitably involve. The new technologies of interactive television and individualised ICT will reinforce this trend, such that provision for non-traditional learners will have to be deliverable in a 'menu driven' format to suit different levels of ability, preknowledge, language skills and different areas of personal interest and circumstance.

In the midst of this picture of change, some aspects of higher education for non-traditional learners will stay close to conventional university practice. The pressure for professional accountability and correspondingly recordable lifelong learning may see non-traditional university provision being increasingly integrated into the universal, and into the mainstream credit accumulation and transfer schemes which are now extending worldwide. This will occur as the obsession with acquiring and comparing educational qualifications continues to grow, and professional life becomes more subject to legislation and litigation. Already, it is debatable whether the continuing professional development courses required of recently graduated architects or medical students should strictly be described as traditional or non-traditional – clearly in order to continue to practise, this journey through a range of post-graduation higher education experiences will become universal and thus quickly 'traditional' in a growing range of professions.

Concluding remarks

In conclusion, it is clear from the range of analyses presented in this chapter that non-traditional learners are here to stay in higher education. Indeed, they are set to increase their influence on a growing number of universities. Each area of analysis turned to by this chapter has placed non-traditional learners at one end of a series of learning/teaching dimensions, but then each analysis has revealed that traditional higher education practice is moving steadily in the same direction. Hence the varied pre-knowledge base, socio-economic and national/international backgrounds of non-traditional learners are increasingly seen amongst traditional first-year undergraduates. Similarly, the flexibility in learning/teaching delivery which was once a hallmark of non-traditional higher education has come into the mainstream, as has its ICT dependence and mobility.

However, the analysis suggests that some features of non-traditional higher education are distinctive and enduring. Its 'adaptive' potential for learning from its characteristically experienced and diverse audience marks it out. The opportunities, but also the pitfalls of growth through 'supply push' projects, hopefully learning from recent e-university difficulties, will remain distinctive in the sector, although 'demand pull' in the growing non-traditional higher education 'market' is also growing. The consequent rebalancing of the population of universities (at least those in the West), will mean that yesterday's young traditional undergraduate will be tomorrow's 'greying' mid-career non-traditional student.

Overall, as nations around the world realise both the societal and the economic advantages of high university participation levels, with 50 per cent being the current UK benchmark, it is likely that non-traditional students will replicate the growth spurt demonstrated by conventional undergraduate numbers at the start of this 30-year review. In particular, theirs may be seen as an alternative higher education experience to the normal recipe of starting adult life via conventional three-year full-time degrees.

Educational policy makers may then start asking whether, if the higher education experience is truly civilising in society, it is a benefit which should primarily be delivered traditionally at the end of adolescence, and if not, how can we ensure that our non-traditional learners gain the maximum benefit from the wider values of higher education.

Part II

The development of learning technologies in higher education

Chapter 6

E-learning in higher education

Diana Laurillard

Introduction

This chapter examines the nature of change in higher education with respect to the introduction and growth of e-learning. While the ostensible aim is to use e-learning to improve the quality of the learning experience for students, the drivers of change are numerous, and learning quality ranks poorly in relation to most of them. Those of us working to improve student learning, and seeking to exploit e-learning to do so, have to ride each new wave of technological innovation in an attempt to divert it from its more natural course of techno-hype, and drive it towards the quality agenda. We have to build the means for e-learning to evolve and mature as part of the educational change process, so that it achieves its promise of an improved system of higher education.

Why is e-learning important for higher education?

A student who is learning in a way that uses information and communication technologies (ICTs) is using e-learning. These interactive technologies support many different types of capability:

- internet access to digital versions of materials unavailable locally
- internet access to search, and transactional services
- interactive diagnostic or adaptive tutorials
- interactive educational games
- remote control access to local physical devices
- personalised information and guidance for learning support
- simulations or models of scientific systems
- communications tools for collaboration with other students and teachers
- tools for creativity and design
- virtual reality environments for development and manipulation
- data analysis, modelling or organisation tools and applications
- electronic devices to assist disabled learners.

For each of these, there is a learning application that could be exploited within higher education. Each one encompasses a wide range of different types of inter-action – internet access to services, for example, includes news services, blogs, online auctions, and self-testing sites. Moreover, considering combinations of applications could further extend the list above. Imagine, for example, a remotely controlled observatory webcam embedded in an online conference environment for astronomy students; or a computer-aided design device embedded in a role-play environment for students of urban planning.

The range and scale of possible applications of new technologies in higher education is almost beyond imagining because, while we try to cope with what is possible now, another technological application is becoming available that will extend those possibilities even further. Everything in this chapter will need updating again when 3G mobile phones begin to have an impact on our behaviour. Never mind; we keep the focus on principles and try to maintain our equanimity in the face of these potentially seismic changes.

E-learning is defined for our purpose here as the use of any of the new technologies or applications in the service of learning or learner support. It is important because e-learning can make a significant difference to how learners learn, how quickly they master a skill, how easy it is to study and, equally important, how much they enjoy learning. Such a complex set of technologies will make different kinds of impact on the experience of learning:

- Cultural – students are comfortable with e-learning methods, as they are similar to the forms of information search and communications methods they use in other parts of their lives.
- Intellectual – interactive technology offers a new mode of engagement with ideas via both material and social interactivity online.
- Social – the reduction in social difference afforded by online networking fits with the idea that students should take greater responsibility for their own learning.
- Practical – e-learning offers the ability to manage quality at scale, and share resources across networks; its greater flexibility of provision in time and place makes it good for widening participation.

There is also a financial impact. Networks and access to online materials offer an alternative to place-based education that reduces the requirement for expensive buildings, and the costs of delivery of distance-learning materials. However, learners still need people support, so the expected financial gains are usually overwhelmed by the investment costs of a new system and the cost of learning how to do it. We cannot yet build the case for e-learning on cost reduction arguments – we are better placed to argue for investment to improve value than to save costs.

Changing higher education towards the use of e-learning

E-learning could be a highly disruptive technology for education – if we allow it to be. We should do, because it serves the very paradigm shift that educators have been arguing for throughout the last century. Whatever their original discipline, the most eminent writers on learning have emphasised the importance of active learning. The choice of language may vary:

- Dewey's inquiry-based education
- Piaget's constructivism
- Vygotsky's social constructivism
- Bruner's discovery learning
- Pask's conversation theory
- Schank's problem-based learning
- Marton's deep learning
- Lave's socio-cultural learning

but the shared essence is the recognition that learning concerns what the *learner is doing*, rather than what the teacher is doing, and the promotion of active learning in a social context should be the focus of our design of the teaching–learning process. It is especially the social situatedness of learning, in the Vygotskyan tradition, that is the focus of David McConnell's chapter in this book.

If the organisation of teaching and learning in higher education were driven by the insights of these scholars, then e-learning would have been embraced rapidly as the means to deliver active learning. But change in higher education requires a subtler understanding of the forces at work, and here Lewis Elton is a valuable guide. In his analysis of strategies for innovation and change in higher education (Elton 1999), he draws a distinction between hierarchical and cybernetic models of governance, which have contrasting approaches to change, the former being top-down, the latter relying on a network structure that allows the opportunity for bottom-up as well. Achieving the right balance between the two enables innovation to be embraced within a model of change management:

> New ways of learning ... require new forms of institutional management.
> (Elton 1999: 219)

So if universities are to rethink their methods of teaching, they need a management structure that is capable of supporting innovation:

> The process of change must be initiated from both 'bottom up' and 'top down', with the bottom having the knowledge and the top the power ... The top must use its power, not overtly and directly, but to facilitate the work from the bottom and to provide conditions under which it can prosper.
> (Elton 1999: 215)

A top-down management structure is inimical to successful innovation precisely because management does not have the necessary knowledge. A similar point is made in a collection of articles in a recent Demos publication on the process of reform in the public services in general. Here the 'mechanistic state' is contrasted with the 'adaptive state' (Bentley and Wilsdon 2003). Again, the point is made that if we try to innovate through command and control methods, the innovative idea weakens as it travels down the hierarchy and confronts the local system knowledge it is failing to use in its process of reform. In an adaptive or cybernetic structure, the model is not a unidirectional graph, but a network, with multiple two-way links between all nodes, even if there is a hierarchical organisational structure. These local dialogues allow localised versions of the innovation to spread downwards, customised versions to spread sideways to peer groups, and generalised versions to travel upwards to managers and leaders.

> We need systems capable of continuously reconfiguring themselves to create new sources of public value. This means interactively linking the different layer and functions of governance, not searching for a static blueprint that predefines their relative weight.
>
> (Bentley and Wilsdon 2003:16)

Another source for this kind of analysis is the literature on knowledge management, which draws our attention to the importance of continual innovation, if an organisation is to remain competitive. Senge's (1993) analysis derives from a systems approach, and concludes that the organisation must be 'continually expanding its capacity to create its future ... "adaptive learning" must be joined by "generative learning" – learning that enhances our capacity to create' (Senge 1993: 14). The quote captures the twin tasks of both generating new knowledge and monitoring existing activities, to ensure adaptive change in response to the external environment. Similarly, Nonaka (1994) made the link between knowledge creation and competition in his seminal paper on organisational knowledge, and his model draws attention to the relationship between individual learning and organisational learning. Organisational knowledge creation is seen as a continual dynamic process of conversion between tacit (experiential) and explicit (articulated) knowledge, iterating between the different levels of the individual, the group and the organisation. Again, the network, rather than the directed graph, is the optimal model for innovation, and the dialogic process between individuals and groups at different levels of description of the organisation is very similar to the principles embodied within the conversational framework for learning (Laurillard 2002: 215ff).

Interestingly, higher education already fosters an excellent model for innovation and progression through a cybernetic/adaptive model of change. The academic research community has perfected a process that fosters the creation and development of knowledge, and that is so effective that its basic characteristics are common to all disciplines. I think it is fair to say that all academic disciplines share a fundamental set of requirements for high quality and rigorous research. The academic professional as researcher is:

1   fully trained through an apprenticeship programme, giving them access to competence and personal engagement with the skills of scholarship in their field;
2   highly knowledgeable in some specialist area;
3   licensed to practice as both practitioner and mentor to others in the field;
4   building on the work of others in their field whenever they begin new work;
5   conducting practical work using the agreed-upon protocols and standards of evidence of their field;
6   working in collaborative teams of respected peers;
7   seeking new insights and ways of rethinking their field; and
8   disseminating findings for peer review and use by others.

In the context of research, academics measure up well to the idea of 'the reflective practitioner' (Schön 1983) working within a 'community of practice' (Wenger 1999). The progress of innovation is rapid and effective.

Now run through the above list again and consider whether the academic professional as *teacher* possesses those characteristics in relation to the field of the *pedagogy of their subject*. None of them, typically, apply. Not even number two, since academics are rarely specialists in the pedagogy of the subject, beyond a simple reliance on expert knowledge.

If there is to be innovation and change in university teaching – as the new technology requires, as the knowledge economy requires, and as students demand – someone has to take responsibility for it. Who should that be, other than the university academic community? Private providers are ready to try; despite the near-universal failure of 'e-university' organisations since the dot.com boom, the private sector is innovative and inventive and will eventually discover how to turn degree-level education into a profitable business. The demand can only increase. The knowledge economy needs employees who are intellectually confident, capable of taking the initiative in information-acquisition, -handling and -generation, and able to take responsibility for their personal development of knowledge and skills. The generation and acquisition of new knowledge is widespread and rapid in a maturing knowledge economy. Students being educated to cope with it must not be sheltered from the processes of knowledge development. We are in danger of doing that if we allow universities to separate research from teaching as a way of coping with the crises of funding and the professionalism of academics. Knowledge creation is not confined to universities, and graduates will be taking part in the generation and communication of both expert and practitioner knowledge as an inevitable part of their professional life. A university education capable of equipping students for the twenty-first century must pay close attention to the skills of scholarship – keeping abreast of existing knowledge, rigorous argument, and evaluation of evidence – no matter what the discipline.

All academics, therefore, need to cover the full range of professional skills of both research and teaching. They will differ in proportion, of course, but there is no easy exit from the responsibility of every university to offer its students access to expert teaching informed by current research, to give them the capabilities they need for their own professional lives.

University teaching must aspire to a realignment of research and teaching and to teaching methods that support students in the generic skills of scholarship, not the mere acquisition of knowledge. Forward to the past: universities have to manage on the large scale the same values, aspirations and modus operandi they used for a privileged elite.

We might expect to conclude, from the previous discussion, that the most productive form of system redesign for innovation in pedagogic style in higher education would be to return to the undirected collegial networks of earlier decades, before top-down management took hold. The technology itself serves that shift because it creates the means by which multiple networks can co-exist, inter-operate, and self-generate. But technology does not yet adapt to major change in a seamless, incremental way. The technological changes we exploit on the grand scale demand giant upheavals in the physical and organisational infrastructure. The motor car prompted incremental changes from lanes and carriageways to tarmac roads, but it also demanded the complex centralised infrastructure of motorways and licensing laws. ICT is making many incremental changes to local ways of working, but it also requires the pooling of resources to create shared networks, and agreed technical standards to enable those networks to inter-operate. These changes do not happen without planning and coordination. The change towards e-learning creates the peculiar challenge that it needs both the network-style 'cybernetic systems' approach to innovation, and the top-down, 'command and control' approach to shared infrastructure and standardisation.

We could position e-learning, therefore, as the means by which universities and academics manage the difficult trick of making the learner's interaction with the academic feel like a personalised learning experience, focused on their needs and aspirations, developing their skills and knowledge to the high level universities always aspired to, while doing this on the large scale. E-learning enables academics and students to communicate through networks of communities of practice in the cybernetic approach that makes change and innovation an inherent property of the system. At the same time, we need a way of creating the common infrastructure of agreed standards of interoperability that enable, and do not frustrate, innovation.

Technological change and the learning experience

The information revolution is sometimes compared with the Gutenberg revolution, when the printing press harnessed a mass-delivery system to the medium of the written word. It is a good parallel to draw for the impact of the internet, but it undervalues the other key feature of the interactive computer – its ability to adapt.

The simple fact that it can adapt its behaviour according to a person's input means that we can engage with knowledge through this medium in a way that is radically different from our interactions with the unresponsive medium of print.

A better analogy for interactive computing than the printing press, to give a sense of the power of this revolution, is the invention of writing. When our society had to represent its accumulated wisdom through oral communication alone, the process of accretion of communal knowledge was necessarily slow. Writing gave us the means to record our knowledge, reflect on it, re-articulate it, and hence critique it. The means by which the individual was able to engage with the ideas of the society became radically different as we developed a written culture. When a text is available in written form, it becomes easier to cope with more information, to compare one part with another, to re-read, re-analyse, reorganise and retrieve. All these aspects of 'knowledge management' became feasible in a way that had not been possible when knowledge could only be remembered. The earliest surviving written text – the Rosetta Stone – shows that 'information management' was an important benefit of the medium, recording the resources available, allowing a tally to be kept, enabling better management of the way the society operated.

The nature of the medium has a critical impact on the way we engage with the knowledge being mediated. The oral medium has the strength of having a greater emotional impact on us which enables action through motivation; the written medium has the strength of enabling a more analytical and reflective approach to action. As we create and generate knowledge and information we naturally use different media, depending on the nature of the content and the objective we want to achieve. It is impossible, for example, to use a verbatim transcript of a lively lecture for a print version. The spoken word written down usually reads badly. Medium and message are interdependent; there is an internal relation between them.

What does the new medium of the interactive computer do that is so significantly different from the earlier media? The written medium had a transformational effect on an oral culture because it enabled the representation, analysis and reworking of information and ideas. These are clues we can use. The interactive computer provides a means for representing information and ideas not simply as words and pictures, but as structured systems. A program is an information-processing system that embodies a working model with which the user can interact – not just analysing and reworking, but testing and challenging. This is true even of the familiar word-processing program. It does not just record the words, as a typewriter does; it also has information about the words – how many there are, how they are arranged, what shape the letters are. Because of that, it can offer options that enable the user to input changes to the system and see the resulting output. We can experiment with layout, font, structure, in ways that are not possible with a typewriter, and are excessively time-consuming with pen and paper. So the adaptive nature of an interactive computer enables enhanced action because it holds a working model with which we can interact to produce an improved output. Graphics programs, and presentation authoring tools, all work on the same principle.

A spreadsheet holds a different kind of working model. It holds not just data but also ways of calculating the data to represent different behaviours of a system. A common application is for modelling cash flow for a business. The user can determine the initial data about costs and pricing, for example, and the spreadsheet calculates the profit. By changing the prices, the user can experiment with the effects on profits. The cash-flow model embodies an assumption about the effect of prices on sales – for example, that they will fall if the price goes above a certain limit. But the user can also change that assumption, by changing the formulae the spreadsheet uses for calculating profits. So there are two ways in which the user can engage with this model of the cash-flow system: by changing the inputs to the model, and by changing the model. The adaptive nature of the medium offers a creative environment in which the user can inspect, critique, re-version, customise, re-create, design, create and articulate a living model of the world, wholly different from the kind of purely descriptive model that can be created through the written word.

These two examples illustrate the power of the interactive computer to do a lot more than simply provide *access* to information. It makes the *processing* of that information possible, so that the interaction becomes a knowledge-building exercise. Yet the excitement about information technology has been focused much more on the access than on the processing it offers. And the most popular technology developments so far have reflected that. The focus has been on the presentation of information to the user, not on tools for the user to manipulate information, nor on environments for learning.

The sequence of technological change in interactive technologies has been a historical accident, driven by curiosity, the market, luck, politics (for a brilliant account of this, see John Naughton's *A Brief History of the Future* (1999)) – never by the needs of learners. Learning technologies have been developing haphazardly, and a little too rapidly for those of us who wish to turn them to advantage in learning. This becomes more apparent if we compare these technological developments with the historical development of other key technologies for education.

Table 6.1 shows some of the main developments in information, communication and delivery technologies over the last three decades, which all help to support learning in different ways, and against each one proposes a functional equivalent from the historic media and delivery technologies. The story begins with interactive computers because this first move away from batch processing brought computing to non-programmers. The user had access to a new medium which responded immediately to the information they put in. As I have argued above, this new medium for information processing was radically different from the much more attenuated relationship between reading and writing, thus creating a new kind of medium for engaging with ideas.

But look at the rest of the story – how rapid the development of new possibilities has been! Each new technological advance brought new functionality and hence a new way of potentially supporting learning. The world of education has responded to all the old technologies, over the centuries, finding ways of incorporating their

Table 6.1 New media and delivery technologies for information processing and communications compared with their functional equivalents for reading and writing

Date	New technology	Old technology equivalent	Learning support function
1970s	Interactive computers	Writing	New medium for articulating and engaging with ideas
	Local hard drives and floppy discs	Paper	Local storage with the user
1980s	WIMP interfaces	Contents, indexes, page numbers	Devices for ease of access to content
	Internet	Printing	Mass production and distribution of content
	Multimedia	Photography, sound and film	Elaborated forms of content presentation
1990s	Worldwide Web	Libraries	Wide access to extensive content
	Laptops	Published books	Personal portable access to the medium
	Email	Postal services	Mass delivery of communications messages
	Search engines	Bibliographic services	Easier access to extensive content
	Broadband	Broadcasting, telephones	Choice of elaborated content and immediacy of communication
2000s	3G Mobiles	Paperbacks	Low-cost access to elaborate content
	Blogs	Pamphlets	Personal mass publishing

functional value into the way we do teaching and learning, and each one has its own history of pioneering teachers, new pedagogies, new business models, new teaching skills, changes in educational institutions and in the politics of education. They have all made improvements in the quality of the learning experience, but it has taken centuries for these changes to be absorbed.

There is one very striking point about Table 6.1 when we reflect on innovation in the digital world: the development in information and communication technologies over the *last three decades* is comparable with the development in information and communication technologies over the *last three millennia*. No doubt there are alternative ways of drafting such a table, but that point at least is likely to be common to any analysis of ICT.

Attempting to construct these equivalences is instructive in itself. It is difficult to represent the importance of computer-mediated conferencing, for example, as there is really no clear historical equivalent to enabling large group discussion across huge distances. Table 6.1 does not cover the full range of new technology forms, but succeeds, nonetheless, in illustrating the extraordinary capabilities of the technologies we are now struggling to exploit. We have to be aware of the impact this fecund inventiveness is having on our intellectual life. The chronological sequence of discoveries obeys no user analysis of learners' needs – electronic inventions are 'created by engineers and computer scientists working in a spirit of enthusiastic co-operation, debugged in the crucible of intensive peer-review' (Naughton 1999: xi) but the sequence matters.

It is an accident of the history of technology, for example, that the glorious presentational media of sound, film and television became available for mass access, in the form of multimedia, so soon after the advent of commercialisation of the interactive computer. It meant that interactive computing, potentially as important as writing, has been unable to develop as a medium for design and creativity. We must be aware that this historical accident affects the user's engagement with the new technology. Whereas most people can write, very few people can create something with ICT. There is no real equivalent of pens and pencils. The focus of new technology development has been on exploiting its multimedia capabilities to give access to presentational media – the equivalents of books, libraries, bookshops, broadcasting, films, television, etc, rather than on the technologies for individual creativity like pens, pencils and notebooks. Because we can write as well as read, there is the opportunity for ideas to build, to be questioned, critiqued, re-used, re-purposed, re-combined, for all of us to take part in a collaborative creative process. For most of us, our creative re-working that utilises new technology is confined to the use of word processing and email systems – the medium of writing made more convenient and with better delivery options. We use the internet to access information, just as we use books, newspapers and television. But most of us do not use it – yet – to design, or create, or take part in a collaborative creative process that mirrors the traditions of writing. The office applications of word processing and email have simply enhanced the medium of writing, rather than opened up a new kind of medium for intellectual activity.

The closest we have come to the equivalent of pens and pencils, the tools that enabled all of us to contribute to the written medium, is authoring tools such as 'Hypercard', which allowed the user to create their own associations between texts and diagrams in the form of hyperlinks, thereby building their own information environment with no knowledge of programming necessary. It was meant to open up the world of personal computing to non-programmers. Sadly it failed, because almost immediately the web arrived, and with it the world of web pages and browsers. It was another historical accident of technology development that was immensely successful at extending even further the salience of the written medium, but gave no opportunity for us to explore how we might ourselves engage as contributors within the new interactive medium. Bill Atkinson's HyperCard gave us creativity, the ability to create the links ourselves, not merely follow the links created for us, and to experiment with some primitive forms of interactivity. More recent authoring tools, which offer 'blogging' opportunities for individuals to create their own weblogs (linking their own commentary to others' web-based material), mark the beginning of a more successful form of personal creative activity. However, as a form of personal mass publishing, they still make the written word predominant, not the interactive transaction.

We have not fully exploited the medium of web-mediated conferencing as a transformational medium for education, in part, I suspect, because it has no historical equivalent. Scholars have always travelled to debate and confer. The commercial pressure to develop highly attractive and usable networked collaborative systems, of the kind that David McConnell discusses in his chapter, has not been sufficient. Perhaps the new fear of travel in the business world will change this, and education will be able to benefit.

Technological change could affect the learning experience in profound ways, but the direction of its actual impact on education depends on the historical accident of the chronolgy of technical invention, and the drivers of business needs and opportunities. The education system has a porr capacity to either drive or respond to such change. Educators have to match the innovative capacity of the engineers by driving the improvements in learning that become possible, if we are to realise the potential of new technology. We need to learn from them. John Naughton asks 'What does the story of the Net tell us that can be useful for thinking about the present?' We could apply his answer to what educators need to do:

> First of all, it tells us something about the importance of dreams. Engineers and computer scientists and programmers are supposed to be hard-nosed, firmly earthed folk. And yet the history of the Net is littered with visionaries and dreamers who perceived the potential of the technology and tried to envision what it might enable us to do.
>
> (Naughton 1999: 265)

The interactive computer offers the potential for a new kind of personal capability as powerful as the change wrought on human understanding by the advent of writing. It could transform the learning experience in much more exciting ways than simply providing access to information and written communications. If we were really to 'envision what it might enable us to do', if we could harness the new technology to the needs of training and education, we would be focusing more on enhancing the personal capacity of learners, and driving technological development in that direction. That is what we consider in the next section.

E-learning in university teaching

E-learning has been used very effectively in university teaching for enhancing the traditional forms of teaching and administration. Students on many courses in many universities now find they have web access to the lecture notes and selected digital resources in support of their study, they have personalised web environments in which they can join discussion forums with their class or group, and this new kind of access gives them much greater flexibility of study. Part-time students can more easily access the course and this in turn supports the objectives of wider participation, removing the traditional barriers to higher education study. David McConnell's chapter emphasises the importance of network technologies for enabling both campus and distant students to learn through social interaction and collaboration. Just as the historical inventions of the printing press, the postal service, and libraries opened up access to and participation in the medium of the written word, these technologies are opening up higher education through its reliance on this form of access to ideas.

E-learning could do more. The interactive computer could be used to give students an alternative to writing as a form of active participation in knowledge-building. It can model real-world systems and transactions, and can therefore create an environment in which learners can explore, manipulate and experiment. The features of the digital environment are fully controlled by the program so that it can be designed to offer as much or as little freedom to the learner as is appropriate to their level of mastery. A simple example is a mathematical model of a well-researched system, such as population dynamics in biology, or unemployment fluctuations in economics. An interactive simulation enables students to explore how the model behaves according to the way they change parameters. The teacher can set challenging problems, such as finding the combination of changes in inflation and exchange rate that produces a sudden rise in unemployment. Students can inspect and experiment, build and test hypotheses, and generate a rich sense of how this model behaves, i.e. how this economic theory works. The teacher could extend this further, as the students become more knowledgeable, by noting that the model fails to account for a recent set of data, for example, and offer a variation in the model which students must then further investigate and interpret in real-world terms. The nature of the intellectual activities they practise through this interactive medium, is importantly different from the process of reading, critiquing, interpreting and articulating that is typical of their work in the written medium. It does not replace it, but it certainly increases their capability in understanding and critiquing an existing theory. Any system that can be modelled in this way, in any mathematically based discipline, is open to interactive investigation of this kind.

In the humanities, there are other kinds of possibility: a design and editing program, for example, enables students to explore the effects of music on audience interpretation of a film scene, with the goal of producing a combination that generates a specific effect when tested with the target audience; students of art could investigate the principles of composition of paintings and collages, with the goal of using them to illustrate how certain visual effects are produced; drama students could investigate the effects of the timing of pauses in a monologue with the goal of 'directing' a given speech to produce their chosen interpretation.

In the social sciences, a role-play model of human transactions can assign roles, tasks and information to different groups or individuals, and process their decisions to simulate, say, political negotiations; students of child psychology could use a video display and editing program to practise their interpretation of video-recorded behaviours, with the goal of presenting their own evidence of a particular interpretation of a child's behaviour.

There is no discipline of academic study whose students would not benefit from this kind of intimate engagement with the concepts, interpretations and theories of their field. It does not displace their work on the written word, but it does empower their engagement with it. A learner who has experimented with ways of manipulating a Picasso collage approaches an academic discussion of cubism with a much deeper sense of how it works as visual representation, than they do when they have only read an expert's thesis. They must do both, because they must learn the much more efficient forms of articulation of an idea that the written word offers. But the written word does not answer their questions – an interactive program can answer how it would look if the guitar section were not inverted ... The interactive medium challenges, excites and empowers the inquisitive learner who wishes to take some responsibility for what they know and how they come to know it. Embedded within a networked collaborative system, for learners to discuss and debate their creations, ideas and discoveries, we would have a truly powerful learning medium. Why are we not doing more to achieve this?

Concluding remarks

Lewis Elton's work touches this argument throughout his career – from his concern with student evaluation, to the role of computer assisted learning, to the importance of staff development, to the role of institutional change, and overall, in his tireless advocacy, on the international stage, of the needs of the learner.

My personal sense of the value of Lewis's vision for educational technology is illustrated perfectly when I remember the first piece of work I did for him, as a newly appointed assistant on his project 'Computers in the Undergraduate Science Curriculum'. His idea was to give students an interactive simulation in which they could investigate the behaviour of an object in free fall with air resistance, and use this to decide the point at which a parachutist jumping under enemy fire should open his parachute in order to minimise his time in the air without crashing to the ground. We worked with a very primitive interactive graphics display to give students the opportunity to experiment with velocity–time and distance–time graphs, to see how the different types of motion, free fall and with parachute, behaved. They were then shown the real-time plot of the parachutist falling, on a distance–time graph, and had to estimate, using their knowledge of the model, when to interrupt the fall and open the parachute. I learned my first lesson of interactive design here: if the wrong answer is more interesting than the right answer, that is the one they will work to produce – the splat of a crashed parachutist, or his destruction by firing, was evidently much more rewarding than the gentle cruise safely to earth. But the form of the interactivity was engaging and challenging, and focused the students' attention on the key parameters and their meaning in a very direct way. That was in 1974. Thirty years later, despite the fabulous advance of the technology, there are surprisingly few real-time inter-active simulation games in education that challenge students in a similar way. This was an application of the interactive computer that fully exploited its poten-tial to change the way learners engage with their subject. Lewis was a genuine pioneer and visionary in this field, as in so many others.

For the educational innovator, who seriously wishes to improve the quality of education and the learning experience, it is imperative that we create an education system that is clear about its values and sets its aims and ambitions high, and that is capable of rapid adaptation to its technological, as well as its social, cultural and political environment. The argument developed over this chapter suggests that we can do this if we exert some influence over the way in which e-learning is used in universities, and direct its power overtly towards the needs of learners.

Change in universities is an aspect of their organisation, and again, the oppor-tunities of the new learning technologies – including all their capabilities for information processing, communications, mass participation, design and creativ-ity – support the kind of system structure that would enable change to be organic and progressive, adaptive rather than mechanistic.

Chapter 7

Sustaining networked e-learning through collaborative pedagogies

David McConnell

Introduction

E-learning is now a major player in all areas of the educational system. Most governments are addressing themselves to the issue of how to take advantage of new technologies in education, and how to implement e-learning. As one example of this, the UK Government has established several important initiatives in e-learning across all sectors of the educational system, aimed at promoting and supporting teachers in e-learning (for example, see DfES 2003b). In the European Union, the status of e-learning has grown enormously in the past few years. It now forms an important element of the practice of transnational institutional collaboration within Europe (Hodgson 2002). A major concern is the establishment of 'best practice' in the field of education, training and distance learning so as to ensure that citizens of the European Union can play an active role in the knowledge economy (Zenios and Steeples 2003). The incorporation of e-learning into education is clearly seen as a fundamental prerequisite in the construction of a dynamic, competitive and economically powerful society (Commission of the European Communities 2000).

The development of understandings of good practice in e-learning must be central to all these initiatives, otherwise we are in danger of promoting a technology-driven approach to e-learning. The UK Government is becoming aware of this, as a recent Consultation Document points out:

> Technology is leading change at a fast pace, with a result that there is too little attention to exploring the new forms of pedagogy made possible by e-learning – teachers and researchers need more time and support if they are to keep pace.
>
> (DfES 2003b: 13)

But very little has actually been achieved in developing 'best practice', or quality, in e-learning, an issue which Diana Laurillard also brings to our attention in her chapter in this book (but see Beaty *et al.* 2002 for one example of how to ensure high-quality learning and teaching in e-learning, and Collis and van der Wende 2002 for an understanding of how to exploit information and communication technologies in learning and teaching).

This chapter will examine some of the theoretical and practical issues we need to consider when introducing networked e-learning (i.e. learning that occurs through networks such as local area networks and the internet) into higher education learning and teaching.

Networked e-learning

Many terms are emerging to describe the use of electronic communications and the internet in education and training. There is a preference for 'networked e-learning' since it places the emphasis on networking people and resources together, whether they happen to be on campus or off campus, in the same country or situated anywhere in the world. Networked e-learning also places an important and central emphasis on collaboration as the major form of social relationship within the learning context. The emphasis is emphatically on 'learning', and not on the technology (McConnell 2000, Banks et al. 2003). In her chapter on e-learning in higher education, Diana Laurillard takes another view on networking when she discusses the importance of networks in supporting change in higher education.

However, the emphasis to date has been on technology rather than on how technology can facilitate learning, particularly through learner-centred and collaborative approaches. The pace of change means that, although the innovative potential of networked e-learning is still unfolding, the education and training sectors already have to make complex decisions about implementation and the commitment of resources.

There are two key ideas underpinning the implementation of networked e-learning (Banks et al. 2002). The first is that interactions between learners in groups are a significant aspect of their meaningful, intentional, planned development. Learners change when they interact with each other and with online resources. This may involve changes in their abilities, attitudes, beliefs, capabilities, knowledge and understanding, mental models and skills (Spector 2000).

The second is that networked e-learning environments can provide a valuable way of supporting such interactions. Web-based and stand-alone software systems that can support group communication are plentiful (for example see Seufert 2000, Bringelson and Carey 2000, and Barajas and Owen 2000). Indeed, the dominant use of the internet today seems to be for communication (Sklar and Pollack 2000).

The focus on group-based learning therefore has a central place in networked e-learning. A substantial amount of research has been carried out into group learning. Studies have looked at problem solving (Duisburg and Hoope 1999, Jonassen and Kwan 2001, McConnell 2002a, McConnell 2005), computer-supported group learning (Brabdon and Hollingshead 1999, Klein and Doran 1999), cooperative and collaborative learning groups (Ross and Cousins 1994, Brush 1997, Collis 1998), and virtual group learning (Stenmark 2002). There are two central findings of studies looking at collaborative learning (Hanson 2003). The first is that collaboration requires a group of people to work together (Harasim 1990, Kaye 1992, Dillenbourg 1999, Lehtinen *et al.* 1999, McConnell 2000, Wiersema 2000). The second key finding is that there should be a shared understanding in the collaborative learning process (Schrage 1990, Roschelle and Teasley 1995, Lehtinen *et al.* 1999).

From this research, we can see that collaboration between learners is of prime importance in networked e-learning. A comparison of what might be called 'traditional' learning with collaborative learning may help in providing some insight into what is involved. Table 7.1 provides a summary of key issues. Whereas we might characterise 'traditional' learning as largely the transmission of pre-defined forms of knowledge (Boot and Hodgson 1987), cooperative and collaborative learning[1] is about engaging the learner in making sense of their learning and in reconstructing knowledge in a social setting. Collaborative learning therefore has an important focus on personal (and in some contexts, professional) development, as well as academic, or purely cognitive, development.

Socio-cultural learning

Learning is often solely viewed in terms of the development of cognitive processes and conceptual structures in the *autonomous individual learner.* Learning is also often viewed as the acquisition of propositional knowledge.

Learning is, however, inherently social and may depend more on particular cultural and social contexts than has often been thought. From this perspective, we can think of learning as a process that takes place in a participation framework, not in an individual mind. Learning is a way of being in the social world, not a way of coming to know (Lave 1988, Lave and Wenger 1991). This change in our perception of learning is leading to a paradigm shift:

> Human mental functioning is inherently situated in social-interactional, cultural, institutional and historical contexts [this] contrasts with approaches which assume that it is possible to examine mental processes, such as thinking or memory, independently of the socio-cultural setting in which individuals or groups function.
>
> (Wertsch 1991: 86)

From the perspective of socio-culturally mediated, situated learning we can ask: 'What social engagements and processes provide the "proper" context for learning?' and 'What forms of co-participation might be required when engaging learners in these forms of learning?'

These shifts in our understanding of learning are producing a fundamental review of how we teach and how we perceive the 'role' of learners. This is leading to important changes in our pedagogical methods and approaches. Networked e-learning, as a new and emerging paradigm, is drawing on these ideas in constructing its epistemological stance.

Table 7.1 'Traditional' and collaborative learning

Traditional	Cooperative/Collaborative
There is little opportunity for learners to take the initiative, to express themselves, and for direct interaction with their peers. They exercise little control over their studies.	Learners are encouraged to take initiatives: self expression is central to their learning. Dialogue and interaction with other learners is very important. The degree of control can vary depending on the particular context – but being able to make decisions about their learning is central.
Not social: classes are not seen as a social unit. Learners are viewed as individuals with no/little social interaction between them. When social interaction is present, it usually occurs in formal (controlled) situations (e.g. seminars). Learners are encouraged/required to work individually and to compare themselves to others.	Classes are seen as social units where individuals have a need to interact. Interaction and cooperation are seen as important sources of learning. Learners have freedom to form their social groupings to further their learning. Learners are encouraged to see each other as collaborators. There is both support and challenge within group work.
Inherently competitive and envious. There is 'zero-sum' learning, with gainers and losers.	Competition is less likely. There is reduced envy since everyone is working for the good of the whole. The reference point is 'self' and not others. Non zero-sum learning where everyone can 'win'.
Learners are treated as undifferentiated similars.	Learners are seen as diverse individuals with a variety of different interests, concerns, needs and capabilities.
Emphasises the static, passive regurgitating aspects of learning.	Emphasises the experiential process in learning: reflective re-thinking and re-phrasing of ideas and problems.
Emphasises absolutist knowledge: • Tutor/teacher is the repository of knowledge • Institution sets learning criteria and judges achievement • Knowledge exists independently of learners.	Emphasises personal knowledge: • Rigorous testing of ideas against relevant experience • Honesty • Drawing personal conclusions in the context of dialogical learning • Alternative ideas always considered • Testing ideas in action • Knowledge is constructed by learners through processes of engaging in discussion with others and attributing meaning to the world.
Development of learners viewed largely in terms of academic development only. 'Development' not viewed as being central.	Development of learners is central: personal, social, moral, ethical development as well as academic development.
Level 1 learning, i.e. learning a body of knowledge.	Level 2 learning, i.e. learning to learn.
'Courses' are based on a syllabus which is organised, defined and packaged by teacher/tutor.	'Courses' based on problems, ideas, interests, needs of learners and tutors. This involves negotiation, planning, decision making, experimenting, rethinking.

(McConnell, 2000: 111–12)

There is a shift from focusing on the purely cognitive to the situated, and from the individual dimension of learning to the social. This is emerging as a debate about the nature of learning. There is a change away from perceiving learning as something that occurs in the individual's mind – where knowledge and skill are acquired as discrete, transferable entities – to perceiving learning as something that takes place in collective, participatory settings which involve 'active knowledge construction emphasising context, interaction, and situatedness' (Salomon and Perkins 1998: 2).

Four possible meanings of this kind of social learning can be discerned:

- *Social mediation*: here a person or a group helps an individual to learn. A teacher may help a student with a particular learning problem. A group may help a member deal with an aspect of their own, individual learning.
- *Social mediation as participatory knowledge construction*: here the focus is on participation in the social process of knowledge construction. 'Social mediation of learning and the individual involved are seen as an integrated and highly situated system in which interaction serves as the socially shared vehicles of thought' (Salomon and Perkins 1998: 7).
- *Social mediation by cultural scaffolding*: here the emphasis is on the use of tools (necessarily socially constructed) in mediating learning. Tools and artefacts such as computers, the web, virtual learning environments such as WebCT and Blackboard, and books 'embody shared cultural understandings'.
- *The social entity as a learning system*: the focus here is on learning that occurs in groups, teams and other collectives (for example the 'learning company' and 'learning communities'). The learning that takes place in collectives concerns the development of that collective, bringing about changes in its underlying values, beliefs, culture and norms. From this we can see that collective entities can and do learn – they can acquire knowledge and understanding collectively, and act on it.

How do individual and social learning relate to one another? Three propositions have been made concerning this relationship (Salomon and Perkins 1998). The first is that individual learning can be socially mediated learning to a lesser or greater extent, a position that acknowledges that all learning is to some degree social, but the degree to which it is varies from situation to situation. The second proposition is that learning can be distributed throughout a group or collective, with individuals participating *as individuals*. Individuals in teams may learn by themselves, but they also acquire skills and knowledge that benefit the group as a whole. The third proposition is that these two aspects of learning (individual and social) develop in 'spiral reciprocities' where the one influences and supports the other (paraphrased from McConnell 2000).

This can have profound implications for how we perceive the meaning of learning:

It is not enough to learn how to direct one's own learning as an individual learner abetted by artefacts such as textbooks. Learning to learn in an expanded sense fundamentally involves learning to learn from others, learning to learn with others, learning to draw the most from cultural artefacts other than books, learning to mediate others' learning not only for their sake but for what that will teach oneself, and learning to contribute to the learning of a collective.

(Salomon and Perkins 1998: 21)

Interaction: the core of collaborative learning?

Fundamental to all of this is the belief that collaboration is important to learning. What kinds of questions are being asked of collaborative e-learning? Dillenbourg *et al.* (1996) suggest three sets of questions that can help us get a better understanding of collaborative e-learning: questions that focus on the effects of collaborative learning (for example, is collaborative learning more efficient than learning alone?); questions about the conditions of collaborative learning (for example, under what conditions is collaborative learning efficient or worthwhile?); and questions about the kinds of interactions or forms of participation that occur in collaborative learning (for example, which interactions occur under which conditions and what effects do these interactions have?). The central role that computers can offer in helping students interact with and model real-world systems is a feature of e-learning emphasised by Diana Laurillard in Chapter 6.

All of the above are important research perspectives, but the question of interactivity is perhaps fundamental among them. Just as cooperation and collaboration require mutual reciprocation to sustain them (Axelrod 1990), so does collaborative learning. Typically this usually takes place in the form of interaction or participation in the communication process. This is a core human behaviour in the collaborative learning setting. Without interaction and participation there is little if any collaborative learning. New media such as discussion groups, virtual learning environments and the Web offer the potential of interactivity. This greater user involvement and user choice of new digital media offers a powerful sense of user engagement (Lister *et al.* 2003) that can be harnessed in educational settings to promote what many now call 'active' learning. In collaborative e-learning contexts, 'interventions' typically take the form of textual communications in asynchronous and synchronous communication environments.

The concepts of 'interaction' and 'participation' have been used loosely and uncritically in discussions about the practice of networked e-learning, and in the literature too. A critical, empirical examination of what actually takes place in these environments is needed for us to fully understand the nature of 'interactivity'. We might be guided in doing this by referring to contemporary media study literature[2] where questions about the nature of interactivity have been posed. Interactivity is thought to be a natural attribute of face-to-face conversation. The question arises: what forms of interactivity occur in Computer Mediated Communication (CMC) settings (McMillan 2002)? Are these forms of interaction the same as those found in face-to-face conversations, or do they have a distinctive and unique character in CMC contexts?

How might we research such issues? Van Dijk (1999) provides a model of interactivity which may help us get a better and more critical understanding of the phenomenon, and may also provide a useful tool for evaluations of, and research into, interactivity in networked e-learning contexts. He suggests that there are four dimensions of interactivity. There is a *spatial dimension to interactivity*, with the possibility of two-way communication, such as action and reaction (and reaction to reactions). There is also a *time dimension to interactivity* that encompasses synchronous and asynchronous dimensions. Asynchronous communication may, in some cases, 'damage' interactivity if there is too much time between action, reaction and reaction to reaction, though I would suggest that the time between interactions may be beneficial in a learning context as it supports reflection and thought. The third dimension is that of *action and control*, where those taking part take control of the communication, allowing role changes (sender and receiver, or initiator and receiver). Finally, there is a *contextual and mental dimension of interactivity*, in which there is a high level of interactivity allowing the emergence of intelligence of contexts and shared understandings. Using this model, we might pose sets of research questions aimed at examining collaborative e-learning along each of the dimensions. The outcomes of such research could help us understand what actually happens in collaborative e-learning, where interactivity is a key requirement. It would help us bring a critical perspective to the much used term 'active' learning.

Designing for networked e-learning

The introduction of new technology raises serious questions about re-skilling people working in higher education (Beaty 1995). The use of technology in learning and teaching is redefining the work of teachers and staff developers (Ryan *et al.* 2000, Banks *et al.* 2002) and library staff (Levy *et al.* 1996). At an operational level, there are a variety of professional development needs (Thompson 1997):

1 Conducting successful online group discussions
2 New class management techniques
3 Managing online commitments with other responsibilities
4 Developing appropriate assessment strategies
5 Changing administrative procedures

It is clear that the professional development needs are wide ranging. Technical skills are required, but there is a complex of other professional needs such as pedagogical and managerial skills and knowledge requirements. What we need is a critical pedagogy of networked e-learning. In this sense:

> Pedagogy represents forms of cultural production and struggle implicated in and critically attentive to how power and meaning are employed in the construction and organization of knowledge, desires, values and identities. Pedagogy in this sense is not reduced to the mastering of skills or techniques.
>
> (Giroux 1999)

A specific example of this is the pedagogical development needs of academic staff working in networked collaborative e-learning contexts. Cooperative and collaborative networked e-learning typically occurs in group settings. McConnell (2000) discusses some of the learning and teaching differences between face-to-face group work and networked e-learning group work. In the networked context the group dynamics are not necessarily the same as in face-to-face contexts. We need to learn how to interpret them in this new environment. We may feel we understand the dynamics of face-to-face group work, but working in networked environments, where the 'bandwidth' of communications is very narrow, produces different dynamics (see McConnell 2005). Teachers and students have to develop skill in working in these conditions and develop an awareness and sensitivity suitable to 'virtual' interactivity where physical presence is not required and where communications occur in asynchronous forums and real-time chat rooms. For example, some teachers often mention that they have less sense of control in these environments. They say it is easier for students to ignore them. If this is the case and it poses a problem for them, then we have to develop strategies for dealing with the issue that suit the particular circumstances of the teachers involved.

Some authors have reported negative results in the implementation of collaborative e-learning. For example, the medium has been described as impersonal (Keisler 1992, Wegerif 1998) and it has been reported to be difficult to engage some students in meaningful and productive work in e-learning environments (Jones 1998, Jones 2000, Tansley and Bryson 2000). Other researchers report that e-learning environments make no contribution to learning (Veen *et al.* 1998), or that there are low participation rates and copying of other students' work without learning from it (Huysman and Gerrits 1998). But others do not agree:

> This is not our experience. It is true that textual communication can be misinterpreted and that care, attention and sensitivity has to be given to textual communications. But when time and attention is given to a course design that develops and maintains a learning community, the quality of the experience can be very satisfying and highly acceptable.
>
> (McConnell 2002b: 76)

But social interaction cannot be taken for granted:

> The first pit fall is the tendency to assume that social interaction will occur just because the environment makes it possible.
>
> (Kreijns *et al.* 2002: 9)

Using new learning technologies will not in itself produce qualitative changes in learning. We have to actively design the learner's experience to make this happen. Various research studies and evaluations have constantly emphasised this. For example, the evaluation of the UK Teaching and Learning Technologies Programme (Coopers and Lybrand *et al*. 1996) and the commissioned review of the potential of the web in distance education in the United Sates (Phipps and Merisotis 1999) state this. A key finding in an Australian study is that:

> The use of a particular information technology did not, in itself, result in improved quality of learning or productivity of learning. Rather, a range of factors were identified which are necessary for successful project outcome, the most critical being the design of the students' learning experiences.
>
> (Alexander and McKenzie 1998: 4)

Cooperation and the initiation and sustenance of social interaction in e-learning environments cannot be left to chance: they have to be designed into any e-learning course or event. Teachers are accustomed to conscious and deliberate planning for the learning of individuals. Similarly, we have to consciously and deliberately plan for learning that is to occur in groups or communities.

In what ways might some teachers have to change their view of learning, and their role as teacher, in order to accommodate these new designs? In collaborative e-learning contexts, the teacher will have to design learning events so that the learner is supported and rewarded for changing their beliefs about learning and their behaviour as a learner. The collaborative learner will have to be encouraged to:

- learn together with others through discussion, debate, questioning, problem solving and supporting each other
- develop their own questions and search for their own solutions
- share resources, knowing that this will be of benefit to everyone
- share the learning task, bringing different viewpoints, skills and knowledge
- cooperate and *reciprocate* cooperation
- not compete: excessive competition leads to self-centred learning
- understand that they can have full and equal access to academic rewards: everyone can win
- understand the educational benefits of group work
- understand that they can 'construct' their own knowledge and will be rewarded for doing so
- tolerate and support multiple perspectives
- enjoy diversity.

Just as the collaborative e-learner has to work in a new way, so too does the collaborative e-tutor. They have to develop new approaches suitable to a practice that supports and rewards collaborative learning. The collaborative e-tutor:

- helps to organise the group
- has good group development skills and good facilitation and intervention skills
- consults with the learners and ensures their engagement in the learning design
- guides the learners
- is a resource provider
- is an 'expert' questioner, helping learners address important issues and questions relevant to their group work
- is a designer of learning experiences (not just content)
- understands how to deal with asynchronous and synchronous learning/discussion
- critically reflects on their own practice, and is able and willing to change their practice on the basis of reflection
- can see the learning potential of a certain amount of 'chaos' in the learning process
- rarely lectures
- has an 'approachable' presence online
- is able to communicate effectively via text – they have a real 'presence' online
- supports collaborative forms of assessment, such as self and peer assessment

Assessing learning in networked collaborative e-learning

Assessment is central to formal educational processes. In networked e-learning there have to be forms of assessment which support and reward learners in processes of collaboration, interactivity and discussion. If we assess collaborative learning in traditional ways, we will undermine the aims of networked e-learning discussed above. Learners are quick to challenge learning designs that focus on collaboration if they are not rewarded for participating in them.

As Vivien Hodgson showed in Chapter 3, collaborative and self and peer assessment methods are now well established in higher education. Their effectiveness and validity have been tested and proven to be acceptable (McConnell 2002b). However, their implementation in networked e-learning is novel and under-developed.

A recent study of the learners' experiences of networked collaborative assessment (McConnell 2002b) indicates three key themes which help illuminate this topic:

- *Appropriateness of collaborative assessment*: learners are very positive about this form of assessment and think it is fair and indeed essential. The online medium, despite some problems, is felt to be appropriate with some positive benefits for the learning process.
- *Collaborative assessment is a learning process*: learners enjoy the benefits of shared insights from a real, and motivating, audience and encouragement to

review and self-assess learning. They give perceptive feedback about affective dimensions of the experience. They also comment on community responsibility, the development of their own skills and their own learning about assessment. Perhaps the most beneficial feature is seen as access to others' work at the formative stage, and the insights into the process of learning and writing that this affords. There is also evidence of a move away from reliance on extrinsic validation of learning towards intrinsic self-validation.

- *Focus for assessment*: learners feel that participation in online group discussions and group work generally should contribute to their assessment. This is acknowledged to be problematic in that the criteria for defining 'acceptable' participation, showing evidence of participation, and demonstrating 'sufficient' participation are each open to question, and could lead to mechanistic approaches if criteria are imposed. This is an issue requiring additional research.

The study indicates that learning relationships have to be fostered, and trust developed and maintained in order for collaborative assessment to succeed. The author concludes:

The outcomes of this research indicate that networked collaborative review and assessment helps students move away from dependence on lecturers as the only or major source of judgment about the quality of learning, to a more autonomous and independent situation where each individual develops the experience, know-how and skill to assess their own learning. It is likely that this skill can be transferred to other lifelong learning situations and contexts. Equipping learners with such skills should be a key aspect of the so-called learning society.

(McConnell 2002b: 89)

Concluding remarks

When I was a research student under Lewis Elton's supervision in the mid to late 1970s, I was always impressed by his willingness to treat me and other research students more as colleagues than just students, and with his genuine concern for promoting learning rather than teaching as the focus of higher education practice. These attributes, among other things, have I think been central to Lewis's practice ever since. They strongly affected me back in the 1970s and have since helped me develop my own beliefs about the central place of learning in higher education and the importance of learning relationships in my own practice, no less so in the practice of networked e-learning.

So I will conclude with some tentative propositions about the educational potential of networked e-learning which in essence are underpinned by a strong belief in the importance of developing learning relationships – between the teacher and students, and between students themselves.

Networked e-learning has a focus on student-to-student collaboration, where students use the technology to learn from and with each other. Students sometimes have difficulty adjusting to these new forms of learning since they are required to move away from an expectation of individualism and competition in their learning, towards one of sharing, cooperation and collaboration. In networked e-learning there is a major focus on constructionist forms of learning, i.e. approaches to learning which involve students learning in a social setting where they construct meaning for themselves from engagement with others, experience and 'making sense' of their struggle to learn. Sharing of resources, ideas and experience is central to networked e-learning and there is a greater degree of openness in the learning process, between the teacher and students, and between students themselves. Computer mediated communications can be used to effectively support online discussions, and existing learning resources can be integrated into networked learning environments. The internet and the web offer rich areas for finding, retaining and using resources useful for learning. In addition, new learning resources developed and produced by students themselves as part of their learning can be also incorporated. In networked e-learning environments, there is great importance in developing *communities* of learners. Finally, collaborative forms of learning help to mitigate against the 'authority' of electronic and other forms of publications, by encouraging students to develop and share their own situated knowledge and learning resources.

Notes

1   For convenience I will use the term 'collaborative' learning to cover both collaborative and cooperative forms of learning. Authors often differ in the meaning ascribed to these terms. The distinction between the two forms of learning usually lies in the way in which learning is achieved: in cooperative learning students work together to support each other's individual learning in the group, while in collaborative learning the group members produce a shared solution to a problem or issue.
2   I am indebted to my research student Mario Hernandez for bringing to my attention literature in media studies which casts light on networked collaborative learning.

Part III

The development of teaching in higher education

Chapter 8

Towards professional teaching in higher education

The role of accreditation

Liz Beaty

Introduction

The move towards a professional status for teaching in higher education has a long and somewhat tortured history. In the past it was accepted that academic staff were appointed as experts in their subject. Student learning was seen as largely unproblematic, with terms such as 'lecturer' and 'tutor' used to denote the teaching–learning relationship rather than the role of teacher. Now academics, and others who support students, are expected to prepare for their teaching role in relation to the process of learning as well as its content. The recent English White Paper (DfES 2003a) gave a commitment for the development of professional teaching standards, with all new staff to be qualified to the standard by 2006, and a similar call was made in Scotland for competence in relation to both the content and process of teaching. However, there is still some way to go before a consensus is reached about what these standards should be and how and by whom an accreditation system should be run. Looking back over 30 years, the issue can seem simple and one wonders what all the fuss has been about, but the changes involved should not be underestimated. This chapter aims to set out some of the history and the underlying arguments along the way towards professional accreditation for teaching in higher education.

Most professional groups have controlled their own move towards accreditation. It has been a form of internal control of standards and, even in some cases, restricting access to professional status as a means of defending the economic value of the work. In other cases the move towards accreditation has been centred on the defence of clients through licence to practise built upon standards of training required before claiming the expertise. In the case of higher education these issues become entangled with issues of autonomy, academic freedom and the relationship between the discovery of new knowledge (which could be characterised as research) and the dissemination of this knowledge to others (which could be characterised as teaching). The appointment of academic staff, their probation arrangements and continued professional development have traditionally been built on their subject expertise and research prowess. The function of teaching students has been seen as a second order function evolving from this primary expertise (Brew 2001).

The issues involved in professional teaching in higher education are complex. They include the nature of higher education and the role of academic staff, the nature and scope of professional development, the target groups for development, the shape of the development and the form of an accreditation process, and the nature of the awarding body. In this chapter, I will explore these issues through an exploration of the policy context and different perspectives on the needs for professional teaching. I will include a short history of phases in the development of an accreditation scheme in the UK, comment on the current state of play and conclude with some aspirations for a longer term and more international future.

The traditional model of an academic

Academics do not readily identify themselves with the word 'teacher'. In fact, until recently some would reject the role altogether, preferring to see themselves as part of a community of scholars where the student's role was to learn and the academic's role was to 'profess the subject'. In this view students are independent and voluntary junior colleagues. Thus in traditional pedagogy, the lecture and the tutorial or 'crit' of students' work places them in an apprenticeship relationship with their professor. The default pedagogy, which worked well where there were low tutor–student ratios, was close to what Wenger (1999) describes as 'situated learning'.

If being able to 'profess the subject' is seen as the essence of the teaching role of academics then professional identity is in relation to a disciplinary specialism. In this perspective, academics see their role as searching for knowledge in relation to this specialist area. Unlike schoolteachers, academics are in the business of discovering new knowledge, of testing the boundaries and critically questioning current ideas. Academic freedom, therefore, is jealously guarded as an essential part of academic life. Thus, the content of teaching and decisions about what is taught has significance as part of the well-guarded right to academic freedom. Some would argue, therefore, that the very essence of higher education is for lecturers to teach whatever they want without censure. It is not the case that academics expect to be able to say whatever they want, but rather that what they teach should not be open to interference, especially political interference. This freedom could be characterised as one of the hallmarks of a democratic society. While school teaching can be seen as part of socialisation, higher education is part of self-actualisation and developing the society of the future (Barnett 1997). This tradition can be seen in the importance academics place on research skills, including argumentation, which bestow on them the ability to use their academic freedom wisely. So, from this perspective, training to be an academic is based on research typically with the PhD seen as the basic qualification for the whole academic role including that of teaching. Even today in the US, and many research-intensive institutions in the UK, it is postgraduates rather than tenured academics who are the focus for training in how to teach. This is not just because they are routinely used as teaching assistants but also because the PhD is seen as the basic training for an academic life. The training is about learning to research the subject and to disseminate it both to other specialists and to students. A consequence has been that training in teaching has been seen as threatening the sacred cow of academic freedom, the essential role of the academic and the very nature of higher education. No wonder the fight to introduce accreditation for teaching has been long and hard.

Changes in social context for higher education

From this starting point, it looks a difficult task to bring training for teaching into higher education, but a number of changes have created a more positive context. The first is the change in the nature of the student body towards a more mass system where degrees are not only an entry into academic life or higher civil service but also into an increasingly diverse vocational future. Graduate professions have developed rapidly in all fields and have sponsored calls for more relevant degrees and different skills bases for graduates. Second, students can no longer rely on a close personal link to professors during their studies; there are too many of them and worsening staff–student ratios have meant that pedagogic forms and course designs have to take the facilitation of learning much more seriously. The diversity of student backgrounds and the fact that many do not enter higher education with academic skills of independent learning also means that they need a better quality of support in order to succeed in the growing demands of a degree course. Coupled with this, the staff of universities, especially since the incorporation of the polytechnics into the university system, come from a more diverse background. The PhD is no longer the gold standard as many academics are recruited from business and professions into vocationally orientated departments where the focus of research and scholarship is more applied (Jenkins *et al*. 2003).

A second contextual factor and linked partly to the growth in student numbers is a new argument for accountability. The increasing amount of public money going into higher education and perceived importance for wide areas of the economy have concentrated the mind of government on the quality of the education offered. The imperatives of value for money and the growing needs of a 'knowledge society' for enterprising and skilful graduates mean that higher education is under scrutiny as never before. While no one would argue against subject expertise as a prerequisite for good teaching, there is now more interest in the quality of the student experience and efficiency of the process. The content of the curriculum may be left to academics when they are basically training the next generation for their own replacement, but moving to a mass system of higher education involves a more hands-on approach of professional bodies, such as the Engineering Council, with legitimate claims on student qualifications and generic 'graduate' skills. So while academics still have a great deal of autonomy about what to put into a curriculum, there is increasing involvement of external agencies and particularly of employing groups in the content and process of degree courses which lead to certain qualifications. Not only the content of the curriculum but also the nature of how it is taught is frequently pre-specified, including the time students spend in supervised practice and the qualifications of their supervisors.

Change has been spurred by a widening of the remit of higher education in relation to social needs. Higher education today is not only about feeding the need for leaders in society but also about providing both generic and specialist bases for all areas of employment beyond manual and lower level service jobs. Higher education is now a commodity required by all who seek a career rather than simply a job. For students, then, the market value of their degree becomes as important as the nature of their experience in studying. Their focus has moved from wanting more choice through a concern with their treatment by lecturers to a focus on the outcome and the comparative value of their degree.

So issues of quality control and accountability to employers and government, as well as to students, are part and parcel of the debate over accreditation for teaching. With this as the context for their introduction, professional standards in teaching may be seen by academics as an imposition rather than as a safeguard of their status. While they may embrace the standards and accreditation requirements of subject-based professional bodies, they are reluctant to see teaching as the defining characteristic of their own worth. From an external stakeholder point of view, however, academics' reluctance to embrace professional standards in teaching simply adds to the mistrust of the 'supply side mentality' of university provision.

The nature and scope of professional development for teaching

A consequence of the new demands on higher education is the spotlight on the need for staff development in relation to the process of teaching. Educational researchers and developers have long been engaged in this focus. Their aims have been to improve the experience of student learning through supporting those who teach in devising courses and using techniques of teaching. Developments in the UK on accreditation for teaching have generally started from this more benign intention but the backdrop of academic status linked to research and the changes in the context for higher education have had profound effects on how they have been able to work and indeed on their own professional status.

For educationalists it is obvious that research into how students learn and innovations in learning technology would require more systematic and intentional staff development for those who teach. With the move towards a mass system the needs of students became more apparent and the need for staff to have the necessary skills was similarly brought into focus. Those who have been involved in the development of accreditation processes and running development courses for staff generally are concerned about the needs of students. From this point of view, it is clear that teachers need to understand pedagogy, learning theory and course design including assessment. The importance of developing professional standards for teaching stemmed from the conviction that academic staff should embrace their role in facilitating learning.

In the following sections I will give a partial and descriptive account of the stages leading up to the current move for professional standards in teaching. This account is supported in many of the other chapters in this book. I will start in the 1970s and must preface my account by making it clear that it will be based on personal experience of involvement and is therefore partial.

A short history of teacher accreditation in the UK

The 1970s–1980s: waking up to the process

What was happening?

As Paul Ashwin showed in Chapter 1, in the 1970s the higher education sector in the UK had recently experienced expansion. The polytechnics were very strong in vocational higher education and many of their staff had been recruited from areas of industry and the public sector related to the courses. So the academic staff, in departments from accountancy to engineering, were more likely to have qualifications related to their profession than a PhD. The sector as a whole took for granted that academics were qualified for their teaching role through being scholarly in their discipline. There was general agreement that an appropriate qualification was either the PhD in traditional subject areas, or in the case of applied vocational areas, a professional qualification and experience were seen as the essential pre-requisite. Nowhere was there a view that academics needed to be trained in the process of teaching. This was expected to be picked up through experience and from working with colleagues and, in general, there was sufficient time for new staff to work themselves in slowly and to discuss issues with their colleagues. Class sizes were small and problems could be worked on as they arose mostly face to face with individuals or small groups. The informal approach to course management went broadly unchallenged because on the whole it worked when students were both highly qualified and unlikely to complain about the quality of their courses. Indeed, students were still generally more interested in international affairs and party politics than the internal politics of university organisation (Silver and Silver 1997), although they were very keen to complain about the cost of residences, and rent strikes were common. The closest students got to complaining about the quality of their courses was if they felt they had restricted choices about what they could study. Parents were not seen as important stakeholders in their children's education in universities, since to gain a place generally guaranteed a good job in the future, regardless of the degree topic or the status of the institution. Fees, paid for by local authorities, maintenance grants and financial help with accommodation in the vacations, meant that most students could feel independent of their parents on going to university. The impetus for a focus on teaching came first from individual staff themselves, generally focused on development of the curriculum and on academic standards, and second from those who were interested in educational research where ideas on different approaches to teaching were beginning to become influential. Some of these were technologically based; others were focused on understanding the student's experience in university.

The developments

As indicated, most staff learnt how to undertake their teaching duties by working within departments and picking things up from their colleagues. There was little formal induction and only a handful of places where courses in teaching were available. One of these was at Surrey University. The Surrey course was five days long and included sessions on lecturing, small group teaching and assessment. It also included new technology through a workshop activity in which, with the support of library staff, participants made a tape/slide show to be used in their teaching. The course was based on a series of lectures, discussion and workshops, and participants were assessed and given feedback on presentation skills. This course typically attracted around 20 participants, most of whom were new to teaching in higher education and all of whom were volunteers (Elton 1977). Those who completed the course were given a completion certificate but this did not have any generally recognised value. It would have been extremely rare in this period for higher education staff to have a qualification in teaching except for those in departments of education where they had been practising teachers in schools.

The issues in focus

Technology has often had a hand in the developing focus on teaching and at this time there was interest in methods of teaching, especially those based around programmed learning, for example the Keller Plan (see Chapter 2 for further details). Technology in the form of overhead projectors was beginning to take over from blackboards, and computers were beginning to be talked about in relation to opportunities for 'teaching machines'. Drill and practice was a feature of many of these programmes and the earliest assertions about student-centred learning were mainly based on ideas of individual difference. The learning theories that were beginning to be in vogue at this time were based on cognitive development, motivation theories and adult learning with some influence from more longitudinal views of student development (for example, Perry 1970). The Open University was beginning to be influential in relation to the design of courses with inventions such as 'in-text' and 'self-assessment' questions demonstrating a focus on the learner alongside the construction of the teaching text.

The idea of providing qualifications for teaching in higher education, however, was only a glint in the eye of a few individuals, the most influential of whom was Lewis Elton. One impetus for change was the growing research into learning. This was concentrated in education colleges but was beginning to find a foothold in a small number of universities with dedicated departments including a focus on higher education, notably Lancaster, Surrey and the Open University. The innovation of a conference focused exclusively on higher education student learning at Lancaster marked an important step. The first of these was in 1978 and attracted an international group of over 200 academics all focused on influencing teaching through an understanding of how students learn. This conference illustrated the development of a cadre of educational researchers who were dedicating their attention to student learning in higher education.

Government level and institutional level interest (except for the Open University) was minimal. Most academics had no access to educational development of any formal kind. Where there were opportunities for professional development in teaching these were always voluntary, marginal activities for the few who were particularly interested.

The major problem was an almost complete disjunction between those researching learning and those who were responsible for teaching. Only in the Open University, through the Institute for Learning and Teaching, was there any systematic attempt to connect the two. The challenge of different kinds of learner, with needs because of their distance from their teachers, spurred much innovation in approaches to teaching from the structure of materials to the nature and organisation of teacher to student interaction.

The late 1980s–mid 1990s: early accreditation schemes

What was happening?

The system of higher education was greatly influenced at this time by the removal of the binary divide between universities and polytechnics. The polytechnics had always focused more on issues of quality teaching and less on research. The move to having an agency for quality, the Higher Education Quality Council, which focused on assessment and enhancement, served to focus institutions on how they could assure the quality of their teaching and the professional approach of their staff. By the early 1990s there was a debate in educational development about how to support the development of new staff through induction and initial training in teaching. Typically universities had a two-day induction course, part of which would be based on teaching and tended to focus on 'how to cope with your first week'. In some institutions, these would be followed by a series of voluntary seminars on issues such as assessment and lecturing. So, from the early small group of educationalists focusing on student learning research, there developed, somewhat separately, a community based around supporting academics at the very beginning of their careers. This focus was based almost exclusively on providing techniques, hints and tips because this was what was demanded by staff in their first weeks of teaching.

The developments

During these years, there was a growing number of publications aimed at helping new staff with their teaching role. The most famous was the *53 Interesting Ways to Teach* series (for example, Habeshaw *et al.* 1989). These books acknowledged the fact that academic staff would put staff development for their teaching role at the bottom of a pile of priorities and that they would have neither the time nor the interest to read theoretical books about learning. These, what I like to refer to as, 'translation texts' focused on the need for generic techniques easily applied to many teaching contexts, simply described and requiring minimal theoretical background. They were in fact built on a great deal of educational scholarship but this was hidden from the reader, who was expected to take this scholarship on trust and focus on whether the ideas worked in practice. The pick-and-mix approach was incredibly helpful and easy to read, although some educationalists were scornful of these 'translations', seeing them as somehow a-theoretical.

The issues in focus

This phase of development was based around the need to help teachers with huge issues around working with large groups of students. The pressures on staff could not be ignored and the answer was seen to be in the dissemination of practical techniques and methods of classroom management, though loosely based on learning research and with the strong intention of maintaining a student-centred focus. It was clear from the success of publications like the *53 Interesting ...* series that some staff wanted practical hints and tips, and this served the market of new lecturers very successfully, even if the learning research underpinning this series was hidden from their view.

The Staff and Educational Development Association (SEDA) accreditation scheme was based on the ambition to help educational developers do two things. First, to gain the resources required to support teachers in learning how to teach through demonstrating a professional standard, and second, to synthesise good practices and experiences across the sector. The SEDA teacher accreditation scheme was a bottom-up development, which over a five-year period had 40 courses accredited. The scheme was named in the Dearing Report (NCIHE 1997a) as the basis on which professional qualification for teachers should be built. The innovation of the scheme was that it specified outcomes rather than inputs around a set of broad competence areas and a set of values. These values are a hallmark of professionalism in other fields and serve to give the resultant courses a professional development focus rather than a skills-based focus. The scheme was also based on the idea, in vogue at the time, of reflective practice as the basis for professional development. By 1997, the majority of universities had some provision for the teaching development of their new staff. They also tended to have identifiable staff employed variously as educational developers, or staff developers, whose job it was to run these programmes. The variation in role designation was often reflected in its institutional place and status: typically, the post-1992 universities recruited developers onto academic contracts and located them in academic centres or departments; whereas many of the pre-1992 institutions either used seconded academic staff from other disciplines or else created academic related contracts for academic staff development within human resource departments.

The growth of a cadre of staff identifying themselves with this role has been one of the important factors enabling teachers' accreditation. Many of these staff were academics in a discipline area and moved into a focus on education, while others were educational researchers motivated by the need to apply their research in practice. Still others came from a more managerial or administrative position in human resources areas. The differences within this group have been both its strength and its weakness. As teacher accreditation has grown in importance, the place of these staff within universities has had a profound interrelationship with its status and acceptability to other academics and university leaders.

One of the first programmes which brought these educational developers together in a deliberate way was the Large Group Teaching Project. This project was funded as one of the last acts of the Polytechnic Funding Council, and paid for a group of educational development consultants under the leadership of Graham Gibbs to produce a set of booklets on teaching large groups and to run a programme of workshops for each university and college in England. The programme was influential in aspiring to have teaching and learning brought into strategic decision-making and it heralded the beginning of a more assertive approach to development, starting not only from the needs of individual academic staff but also from the needs of an institution to develop teaching and learning approaches to fit the new context of mass higher education.

At the beginning of the decade academic staff were likely to argue that they did not teach but rather professed their subject and would assert their individual right to specify the values against which good teaching could be judged. By the end of the decade there was much more acceptance of the idea that teaching involved skills and methods that could be learnt and that teacher development should be supported. There was also more acceptance of the language of educational development such as reflective practice, deep and surface approaches to learning and the acknowledgement of individual differences in learning. However, there were also the beginnings of a visible backlash against the generic, rather than subject specific, focus and the perceived lack of scholarship underpinning some teacher development courses.

While the idea of professional training for a teaching role was beginning to be acknowledged, it was by no means a universal provision. The most vociferous criticism was against the notion that teaching in higher education should be accredited against occupational standards with competencies that were articulated though a complex and tight specification. The rejection of this approach was useful in setting the limits for establishing courses on professional development and in building a consensus. By the time the Dearing Report (NCIHE 1997a) was published, case law was building for a professional development course for new academics consisting of a part-time course over one year, based on generic teaching skills and a base level of scholarship for understanding student learning. The SEDA accreditation scheme at this point had 48 universities and colleges running accredited programmes.

1997–2001: government takes an active interest

What was happening?

The Dearing Report (NCIHE 1997a) was the culmination of a long struggle to gain respectability for the world of educational development. It also saw the birth of a new organisation specifically designed to be a professional body for teachers in higher education, the Institute for Learning and Teaching in Higher Education (ILTHE). The ILTHE set out to have a membership consisting entirely of those who had gained professional qualifications in teaching and to accredit programmes within universities that led to this standard. It took the work of SEDA, the staff development mandate of the Higher Education Staff Development Agency (HESDA), and the neutral stance of the academic unions to develop a course-based and an individual entry route. ILTHE members could carry initials after their name to indicate their professional standing. But the ILTHE was, to some eyes, strangled at birth by the need to gain members in order to be financially viable while at the same time having the mandate to restrict entry to those who were adequately qualified. It was also severely curtailed by the fact that this was a purely voluntary exercise. Neither institutions nor individuals had much inducement to take part. There was no funding to reward those who gained entry (rather the opposite since there was a financial cost to being a member) and there was no government requirement for professional standards in teaching. Some institutions nevertheless gave strong backing to the new organisation through paying for their staff to become members and most universities developed a course that met the accreditation standards for the ILTHE.

The issues in focus

The issues in the 1990s were about who should set the standards for professional teaching. Various subject groups within higher education began to assert their right to be the focus for development. Benchmarking and quality assessment were important background processes. Peer observation of teaching and appraisal systems put the focus clearly on human resource issues and institutional focusing of development. So, from a beginning in the 1970s with the focus on student learning research and the early 1990s' focus on educational development, the late 1990s brought a concentration on managerial and staff development. At this time, institutional processes for development of all staff dominated the hitherto primary position of academics. The nature of higher education change was to focus attention on a wider range of staff who supported the learning experience, on different institutional missions and on issues of change management.

An example of this can be seen in the issue of information and communications technology. The connection of learning technology with educational development has been a feature of at least the last 40 years. From the overhead projector to distance learning and the World Wide Web, technology has both offered opportunities and necessitated change in teaching and learning. In the 1990s, a group of staff variously seen as learning technologists began to develop a presence. They were often located alongside educational developers and in many places fused a connection with librarians so that libraries transformed themselves into Learning Resource Centres. The multi-functional approach to the provision of a learning environment gave a challenge to the nascent accreditation systems which had to find ways to accommodate various groups beyond new academic staff including some who were not naturally seen as academic. One early precursor of this development could be seen in the EduLib project which produced distance learning courses for librarians focused on their teaching function and was accredited by SEDA for Associate Teaching Accreditation as early as 1994. By 2003, both SEDA and the ILTHE had associate programmes which covered postgraduate students, librarians, learning technologists, research supervisors and others alongside the more central new academic staff.

During the 1980s the quality assessment of teaching at subject level had a strong effect on teaching. The requirement to produce handbooks, teaching materials and to be observed teaching with the culmination of a score on six aspects of teaching quality had the effect of focusing institutional management on staff development in a new way. Although there were many complaints about the burden of the assessment process and arguments about the particular focus, nevertheless subject assessment did two things to consolidate interest in teaching. First, it produced a natural sharing of good practice through the large number of people involved in assessment panels and the reports that were written to draw out areas of good practice and areas for improvement within disciplines. Second, academic staff learnt to use the language of learning outcomes and to discuss the rationale for their course design and assessment strategies within teaching teams in ways that would have been rare previously. Together with the development of benchmark standards, again undertaken sensitively through peer groups, this created a readiness in the sector generally for discussions about professional standards.

Alongside the growth of sophistication in educational quality systems has come a new sophistication in pedagogic research that starts from a discipline base. From the early beginning of the Student Learning Conferences, where educational researchers led projects within subject areas, the Scholarship of Learning and Teaching (SOLT) has developed via project funding and increased support for research linked to educational development (see Lorraine Stefani's chapter for further discussion of the scholarship of teaching). This research is often castigated from one side for its reliance on cases that cannot be generalised, while the more pure educational research is criticised from the other side for being irrelevant to teaching practice. Nevertheless, through conferences dedicated to work within the disciplines, there are the beginnings of a new focus for applied educational research that can affect practice and support the professional development for higher education teaching.

2001: professional standards and rewarding teaching

What was happening?

In the recent few years there has been more money given to institutions directly for the development of teaching. The Teaching Quality Enhancement Fund (TQEF) for the first time provided an incentive for universities and colleges to earmark funds for educational development. The money, given at institutional level for strategies in particular, allowed more attention to be given to those who saw their professional role as supporting teachers in developing themselves and their approach to teaching. Educational developers started to have influence within their institutions at a strategic level because they were able to offer funding for development and, unlike the earlier development project funds, these developments were harnessed to institutional level change.

The ILTHE had started to recruit larger numbers of staff through both the institutional route and the experienced route so that a few universities leading the way were beginning to move toward 100 per cent qualified in teaching. Most however were very far from this with new staff having to do courses but most experienced staff carrying on as usual. Although there was an increasing number of academics actively engaged in the development of teaching through national programmes, networks and projects, for most staff continuous professional development in their teaching role was an aspiration rather than a reality.

There has been an increased differentiation of those who contribute to teaching. 'Teachers' now include, for example, work-based learning supervisors as well as campus-based staff. There is a widening of the perspective on professional development from an obsession with new staff training to an acknowledgement of the importance of continuous professional development, not least because the world of learning and teaching in higher education is complex and changeable. Issues of importance now are the needs for widening participation and consequent focus on access and retention. A focus on student as client will be of increasing importance as variable student fees influence the market for higher education.

Employability is again in focus, through the call for more integration between academic, business and social worlds via work-based learning (foundation degrees being the latest of course design developments), the increasing importance placed on employer needs within a higher education system aspiring to a 50 per cent intake, and the importance of an enterprise culture with graduates being encouraged to develop new businesses for themselves. So, at the very time that professional standards are being developed for teaching in higher education, what and who these relate to is becoming increasingly complex.

Another aspect of this complexity is the call to higher education institutions to specialise. The Research Assessment Exercise has been variously blamed for an over concentration on research to the diminution of teaching. There have subsequently been recent calls for more explicit rewards for teaching to rebalance the effort of academics. The recent English White Paper (DfES 2003a) therefore has earmarked money for teaching to be distributed as part of the human resources allocation specifically for rewarding excellent teaching, and a new programme for identifying centres for teaching excellence and rewarding staff related to the centres worth more than £300 million over five years is currently underway. These changes add to the Teaching Quality Enhancement Funding (TQEF) which for the past six years has paid for the Learning and Teaching Subject Networks (LTSN), the National Teaching Fellowship awards (NTFS) and for institutional learning and teaching strategies funding. The institutional level funding has allowed many universities to put on teaching and learning conferences for their staff and to pay for specialist staff, often in each faculty, whose job it is to mentor colleagues on learning and teaching. There is a live debate now about the interrelationships between teaching and research, the importance of pedagogy and how this impacts on the issue of professional standards for teaching, and about the positive effects of teaching on the quality of research.

The chapter by Lorraine Stefani in this book describes the importance of a scholarship of educational development to the process of taking teaching seriously within higher education. In her chapter, Lorraine shows how the scholarship of teaching has developed and how it now integrates with the programmes of funding that support the recognition and rewarding of effective teaching.

A forward look: accreditation within an international perspective

In the US there is a long tradition of focus on the quality of postgraduate students' training and any move to further professionalise teaching would no doubt begin with this group. The US however has a more federal structure with different states having different legislative and funding arrangements with their higher education institutions, so while educational development is well developed in many institutions, there is no government line on accreditation. In Canada the focus of much development has been led by a group of award-winning academics who have published an ethical code for higher education teachers (Murray *et al.* 1996). Like SEDA, the Society for Teaching and Learning in Higher Education is an educational development organisation focused on supporting academic practice. The focus of development is in-service continuous improvement and not professional standards for new entrants to teaching.

The UK remains in the lead for development of an accreditation of professional teaching in higher education, although many other countries especially in

Europe are now very active. In Finland, in 1998, a conference brought together an international group to discuss the developments at the time when few countries had staff training for teaching in place. For many years, the SEDA teacher accreditation scheme was the only one of its kind and was used in other countries as a pilot for local developments. SEDA-accredited programmes were developed beyond the UK including in Hong Kong, Singapore, Sri Lanka, New Zealand and Australia. There is now movement, albeit at different paces, towards accreditation in other countries.

It is safe to say that the rationale for developing professional teaching standards has never been so clear. As I write, there is a new consultation on professional standards for teaching that has been jointly published by Universities UK (UUK), the Standing Conference of Principals (SCOP) and the four funding councils in the UK. It asks for comments on a framework that will allow the Higher Education Academy (which has replaced the ILTHE) to take forward discussions towards a set of professional standards. If the timetable is met there will be professional standards drawn up for 2005. Those who teach in higher education will have available to them an agreed accreditation framework shortly thereafter. If it is successful, it will build on past and current practice, be inclusive, forward looking and create an identity for all those who care passionately about the effectiveness of higher education for students. It will also need to look to an increasingly internationally mobile workforce. A similar development is about to be launched in Australia and it will be interesting to see if this is an early trend in an international movement to professionalise higher education teaching. The earlier discussion has demonstrated the complexity of the issues and I suspect that currently different countries would focus on the issue from different starting points. The developments in the UK may have most immediate influence in Europe where there are moves for a common quality framework linked to the Bologna process. Thus far the focus of this is on course structure but it would be a short leap to focus on the qualifications of staff.

The quality of higher education is defined internationally by the link between research, teaching and professional practice. Teaching in higher education requires scholarship in relation to both content and process. Thus professional standards for teaching must include adequate qualification in relation to the subject, how it is applied and how it is learnt, as well as an ethical code of conduct to include awareness of the legislative framework of public sector organisations. The new Higher Education Academy must therefore fuse together an accreditation framework for generic and subject-based knowledge and skill for higher education teaching including continuous professional development underpinned by educational research and ethical values. It needs to work with and on behalf of the higher education community for the well-being of students and society. It has a lot to do, but it has a firm foundation built over many years on which to base its mission.

Chapter 9

Towards a shared understanding of scholarship in the classroom

Lorraine Stefani

Introduction

In the rapidly changing face of higher education, there are increasing pressures on faculty with respect to providing an effective teaching and learning environment for all students. At a global level, the situation for staff in higher education has become increasingly complex. There are for example: the demands associated with wider levels of participation in higher education necessitating a shift from the rhetoric of student-centred learning to the development of a greater understanding of what it means to design, develop and deliver an 'accessible curriculum' for a diverse student population (Stefani and Matthew 2002). The complexities of the knowledge explosion and growth in the use of Communications and Information Technology (ICT) in teaching and learning require faculty to shift their focus towards enabling the development of key skills essential to student learning to include more emphasis on information literacy and other skills appropriate to learning via alternative media (Breivik 1998). The uncertain dynamics of the long-term needs of the employment market for graduates and of the skills that graduates should possess provide an imperative for ensuring that a major focus of higher education must be to enable students to develop the skills essential to lifelong learning. In addition to these factors, there are the additional issues relating to changes in the level and sources of funding of both institutions and students, and greater levels of scrutiny and accountability regarding both the use of resources and the quality of educational provision.

With this ever-growing agenda, there is little doubt that there is increasing demand for a higher education system that is more relevant to the national economy, and a call for changes in the ways that universities, both corporately and individually, approach what is arguably their most important task, i.e. teaching (Elton 1999).

It is against this backdrop that the concept of the 'scholarship of learning and teaching' is currently a highly topical issue, with some researchers professing that the significant pedagogical concerns that face academics will not be resolved until a more scholarly approach is taken in the development of teaching staff (Lueddeke 2003).

A key question to be addressed, however, is: do faculty fully understand what it means to take a scholarly approach to learning and teaching? The remainder of this chapter will focus on current definitions of scholarship; how scholarship is understood at different levels within institutions; the range and depth of pedagogical developments associated with the 'scholarship of teaching' and how the scholarship of learning and teaching can be more widely promoted.

Defining the scholarship of teaching

Ernest Boyer is often credited with being the originator of the current debate about the scholarship of teaching. His now famous report, *Scholarship Reconsidered* (1990), continues to receive considerable attention. Boyer argued that the natural-science view of the university, deriving from the Germanic Humboldt tradition of learning, over-valued pure research which in turn led to the devaluing of work related to teaching and learning. He rightly commented that 'research and publication have become the primary means by which most professors achieve academic status and yet many academics are in fact drawn to the profession precisely because of their love of and enthusiasm for teaching or for service' (Boyer 1990: 5–6).

In his efforts to persuade us that it is time for faculty to break out of the tired old 'teaching versus research' debate and define in more creative ways what it means to be a scholar, Boyer proposed four different categories of scholarship:

- The scholarship of *discovery*, which essentially encompasses what we understand in higher education to mean 'traditional', discipline-oriented research, research supervision, pedagogic research and managing research.
- The scholarship of *integration*, which means generating connections within disciplines and between disciplines, helping students to make essential connections across the curriculum and educating non-specialists about new insights.
- The scholarship of *application*, meaning to link research and development, to link theory and practice, and practice with theory and knowledge transfer.
- The scholarship of *teaching*, encompassing initial preparation for teaching in higher education, appropriate continuing professional development (CPD), accredited CPD, the role of academic guilds and evidencing the scholarship of teaching.

While Boyer's report has gained esteem and recognition, other researchers have elaborated particularly on the definition of the 'scholarship of teaching'. For example, Shulman (2000) introduces the term 'fidelity' and further describes four kinds of fidelity as being critical to the scholarship of teaching: fidelity to the integrity of the discipline or field of study; fidelity to the learning of students one is committed to serve; fidelity to the society, polity, community and institution in which one works; and fidelity to the teacher's own identity and sense of self as scholar, teacher, valued colleague or friend (Gordon *et al.* 2001). In other words, Shulman opens out Boyer's definition of the scholarship of teaching to take account not just of teaching, but also of student learning and to place importance on and respect for the culture within which higher education teaching and learning occurs.

In the United States a major programme promoting the scholarship of teaching, the Carnegie Foundation's Academy for Scholarship in Teaching and Learning (CASTL), seeks to reinvigorate education by renewing the connections between teaching and research and fostering forms of reflection and inquiry relating to teaching and learning. Of its mission, it states that:

> foundation programmes seek to foster forms of reflection and inquiry that will raise the level of attention to educational issues throughout American life. The long term goal is to stimulate a fundamental shift in values, cultures and priorities of universities ... a shift which in turn, makes possible a reframing of the teaching professions.
>
> (CASTL 2000: 7)

From the above commentary on, current interest in and definition of 'scholarship' as applied to teaching and the educative process, set against the backdrop of the changing nature of higher education, it is obvious that there are serious attempts to redress the balance in terms of the purpose of universities. There is a need to recognise that a major role for academics is to provide the best possible learning experiences for students. This should be an activity that is recognised and rewarded as opposed to the focus being primarily on achieving excellence in disciplinary based research.

However, there are misgivings regarding the interpretation of 'scholarship of teaching'. It may be trendy to use the term, but the danger is that if there is no interrogation of the term, no collective and definitive efforts to explore what the term means, then any activities associated with teaching and learning might be considered to be 'scholarly'.

For example, from the literature on scholarship, different perspectives emerge. One such perspective parallels traditional notions of scholarship as the discovery and advancement of knowledge. As applied to the scholarship of teaching, this would mean that faculty would publish on pedagogical topics in familiar, academic ways, but the question of whether these 'scholars' are in fact effective pedagogues, with a deep understanding of the 'craft' of teaching, and the complexities of student learning would not necessarily be the issue because instructional excellence would be assumed (Weimer 1997).

Despite such misgivings, there does appear to be a growing view, if not consensus, which recognises the need for a reflective approach to the facilitation of student learning, an ability to learn experientially about learning, and a knowledge and understanding based on an underpinning body of pedagogical research. Kreber and Cranton (2000) elaborate on this notion of the scholarship of teaching, suggesting that it includes both ongoing learning about teaching and the demonstration of teaching knowledge. Their model of scholarship includes instructional, pedagogical and curricular knowledge.

While the dialogue amongst researchers regarding definitions and understandings of the scholarship of teaching continues to flow, it is important to remember that 'scholarship' is an active process. While the debate on definitions continues, what actions are being taken within institutions to promote the scholarship of teaching and how does faculty interpret 'scholarship' and 'scholarly teaching'?

The next section will explore emerging views on scholarship and the pressing need to promote and encourage a scholarly approach to teaching at classroom level.

Emerging views on scholarship

In an article on the scholarship of teaching, Middleton (1997) considers that discussion of scholarship, as relating to teaching and learning, is not high on the national agenda, and that the reason for this may be that in essence we delude ourselves into believing that our teaching must be good, because we consider that it is important and we are dedicated to the well-being of our students.

We must ask ourselves, of course, if a dedicated teacher working within the limits of his/her experience, with little knowledge and understanding of pedagogy, is necessarily a good teacher or facilitator of student learning.

However, Middleton (1997) goes further in his article and raises the issue of the supremacy of research. In doing so he touches on the raw nerve of values and rewards in higher education. In most developed countries, the higher education system works in similar ways: faculty are recruited on the basis of their excellence in traditional, disciplinary based research. In the UK system, for example, in many universities with aspirations to achieve excellent research ratings, it is unusual for candidates for academic positions to be asked to demonstrate any understanding of learning and teaching. The message is clear, if not articulated, that teaching is viewed as a second-rate activity and that the expectation is that academics' intellectual efforts should be directed towards disciplinary based research (Rowland 2000).

In the UK, the Research Assessment Exercise, the purpose of which is to enable the higher-education funding bodies to distribute public funds for research selectively on the basis of quality, has in many academics' view added to this perception of learning and teaching being a secondary activity.

This negative perception of scholarship relating to learning and teaching is, in general terms, affirmed when promotion procedures are interrogated. In the UK, it may be the case in the post-Dearing era (NCIHE 1997a) that some universities have made strenuous efforts to show that staff can be promoted to senior academic level on the basis of the 'scholarship of teaching' but there is still little doubt that a candidate with substantial evidence of a strong 'traditional' research record can gain promotion regardless of the quality of any other activity. For a long period of time, the issue of rewards for excellence in teaching activities was relegated to a back-seat position because it was argued that there was no reliable method of judging excellence in teaching that was as simple, as apparently objective, and as apparently credible as that used for judging traditional research (Elton 1999).

While, clearly, the history and development of universities has tended to favour research over teaching as the key indicator of the 'successful academic' (Elton 1995) there may also be, as mentioned above, a subliminal sense amongst many academics that excellence in teaching is not worthy of the same status as research because these same academics delude themselves into believing that they are excellent teachers because they are excellent researchers. In other words, teaching students is not considered to be a scholarly, researchable activity (Stefani and Elton 2002). Little wonder then in this scenario that it has proved problematic to provide incentives and rewards for excellence in teaching.

Evaluating or judging excellence in teaching is problematic if the main tools for such evaluation are teaching questionnaires, most of which are not designed to take account of student learning but rather 'student satisfaction' (Ramsden 2003). Ratings by students cannot generally be taken at face value because students' views on what constitutes good teaching may be based on their favoured means of learning, which might be to be provided with a 'good set of notes' for the purposes of reproducing information. Staff making strenuous efforts to engage students in 'deep approaches to learning' may not be so highly evaluated, in essence because they are taking a scholarly approach to facilitating learning (Trigwell 1995).

The recent increased level of interest in and attention to the 'scholarship of learning and teaching' is a response to the increasingly complex environment within which higher education operates. For example, do we really believe that we can constantly fall back on 'traditional' methods of course delivery in the context of mass higher education and widening participation? Can we hope to get away with repeating, like a mantra, in institutional mission statements, for example, that we are dedicated to the development of a student-centred ethos of teaching and learning and that we respect the diversity of our student population, without interrogating what terms such as 'student-centred learning' and 'diversity' actually mean for us in relation to our classroom practice? Can we truly make effective use of developing technologies to support teaching and learning if we do not think through the pedagogical issues associated with using these new technologies? (See, for example, Littlejohn and Stefani 1999, Fallows and Bhanot 2002.)

Scholarship as applied to learning and teaching should of course always have been an essential attribute of academic staff, but increasingly it has become essential to our survival. There is an urgent need to promote a re-conceptualisation of teaching and facilitation of student learning to recognise that our practices should be theoretically informed, critical and interdisciplinary activities, rather than simply processes of transmission of new knowledge and information, practical activities, or crafts that can be learnt through familiarity without undue intellectual or theoretical effort (Boyer Commission 1998).

To achieve a re-conceptualisation of teaching in higher education and to promote scholarship in the classroom, it is likely that staff roles and responsibilities need to be more clearly defined and that staff will require support and appropriate professional development to assist them in engaging in such scholarship. According to Gordon (1998), it is likely to be the case in future that for many members of staff, there will be more of a clustering of roles. Examples of this clustering might be core staff acting as managers of learning, managers of professional development, overseers of quality systems and leaders of curriculum development. Such clustering of roles would further highlight the need for and appropriateness of scholarship, not restricted to the scholarship of teaching but including the scholarship of discovery, integration and possibly application. Such shifts in roles, or rather reviewing and rationalising the roles of academics, will inevitably impact on the professional development strategies and the role of professional development units within higher education institutions.

There is a need therefore to re-examine the work of professional development units and ask the question: do faculty developers actually embody the principles of scholarly practice as proposed by Boyer? Are all developers engaged in 'discovery' in terms of their own research, and in 'integration' in terms of using the pedagogical research to inform and underpin the work they do with colleagues (Asmar 1999)? The issue emerging here is that it potentially undermines 'scholarship' to provide 'developmental opportunities' facilitated by non-academic staff.

This then begs the question: how do the staff in professional development units themselves conceptualise the scholarship of teaching and how do they promote this across the university? A recent publication on the Scholarship of Academic Development (Eggins and MacDonald 2003) provides a timely contribution to the current debate on whether academic/educational development constitutes a discipline in its own right or whether it constitutes merely a 'set of tools' with which faculty can 'improve' upon current scholarly practice relating to the student learning experience in higher education. Essentially, publication of this book is testimony to the fact that a scholarly approach to learning and teaching requires a scholarly approach to faculty development.

The next section further explores educational developers' conceptions of the scholarship of teaching, drawing on a research and evaluation project funded by the Higher Education Funding Council for England (HEFCE).

Educational development: a scholarly approach

If encouraging and promoting the scholarship of teaching is a key role of educational or academic development units, it is essential to understand the remits and the ethos of these units. While Gosling (2001) and Gosling and D'Andrea (2002) have carried out extensive research on the changing role of educational development units, there is still a sense that 'educational development' is not necessarily always valued by the staff such units are intended to 'develop'. Briefly, educational/academic development can be interpreted to mean the systematic and scholarly support for improving both educational processes and the practice of educators (see, for example, Webb 1996, Stefani 2003). The question to be asked therefore is: do educational developers and educational development units operate in a manner that promotes the scholarship of teaching, across the disciplines?

There has often been criticism of the role of educational development units because the 'fidelity' of the discipline is not always taken into account and because the 'developments' that are promoted are, in general terms, generic. This stance therefore suggests that teaching and learning are largely generic activities (Rowland 2000) but differences in academic background are bound to shape the ways in which academics conceptualise their teaching activities (Becher and Trowler 2001). Recognising this and valuing the insights, concerns and epistemological assumptions that are particular to the different disciplines, Jenkins (1996) argues that an effective context for educational/academic development is with colleagues working from within their disciplinary perspective. This may be translated to suggest that rather than offering primarily generic CPD opportunities, educational developers need to act as facilitators within any disciplinary base, working in partnership with faculty in a disciplinary context.

An example of this mode of working is at the Centre for Academic Practice at the University of Strathclyde where the educational developers respond to requests for support from disciplinary based staff relating for example to curriculum design and delivery. A period of discussion and negotiation occurs during which the developers must work towards an understanding of the nature of the discipline. A cycle of action research (Zuber-Skerritt 1992) ensues whereby the developers act as observers of current classroom practice and support key staff in reflecting on their teaching and their students' learning with the intention of enhancing practice in accordance with pedagogical theory. A major aspect of this means of working is that academic staff are encouraged to take ownership of further cycles of development (Stefani and Nicol 1997). Working with disciplinary based staff and students in this way allows for a scholarly approach to learning and teaching and, in accordance with Shulman's proposition, recognises the fidelity of the discipline and fidelity to the mission of supporting and enhancing student learning. This means of working also ensures impact at departmental level, and is a means of maximising the potential of educational development units.

Further insights into how educational/academic developers conceptualise and promote scholarship was obtained from the outcomes of a HEFCE project intended to lay the foundations for capacity building in higher education with respect to the scholarship of teaching (Gordon *et al.* 2001).

For the purposes of obtaining information on how educational developers across the UK interpreted the scholarship of teaching, a questionnaire was developed to explore current conceptions of the relationships between pedagogical development, research and scholarship, and what activities such terms embrace.

A summary of the responses obtained from over 40 heads of educational development units indicated that the interpretation of pedagogical development is 'the scholarly interrogation of taken-for-granted teaching and learning practice with the intention of moving closer to classroom practice that is research/evidence based' (Gordon *et al*. 2001: 38). According to the information obtained from the questionnaire, the activities commonly associated with 'pedagogical development' in general comprised two key elements: on the one hand, processes of innovation in the activities of the teacher in the classroom which are intended to encourage independent learning, and on the other hand, pedagogical development was interpreted to include the intellectual development in teachers' thinking about, and understanding of, their own teaching and their students' learning.

In this same study, pedagogical research was referred to by some respondents as the next stage on from reflective practice in the classroom, undertaking, for example, qualitative research to inform policy development with respect to teaching, learning and assessment, while others suggested that pedagogical research should be about opening up new ideas and new practices to reflect emerging needs, styles and modes of teaching and learning, thus requiring individuals to critically reflect on their own practice.

What is considered problematic, in terms of approaches to pedagogical research and scholarship, is:

> the expectation that it can fit neatly in with the scientific notion of research which is designed to prove an hypothesis by using an 'accepted' methodology. Whereas in fact teaching and learning research should draw on research paradigms more akin to those employed in sociology, psychology and philosophy.
>
> (questionnaire respondent cited in Gordon *et al*. 2001: 41)

According to the research report, the scholarship of teaching is often interpreted as

> the active seeking of information about teaching and learning by an individual teacher, with the intention of expanding their knowledge and applying it to their own teaching practice. It includes carrying out their own action research or being informed about the pedagogical research of others in general and disciplinary-based areas.
>
> (Gordon *et al*. 2001: 41)

Many respondents in this study felt that scholarship as applied to teaching was stifled both by the spurious belief that it can be easily equated with 'results' as in a scientific research paradigm and also by the lack of esteem afforded such activities.

While the research outcomes here focus primarily on the views of educational developers, it is not always easy to evaluate the overall impact of 'development' on faculty. The next section summarises the understandings of scholarship as applied to teaching as determined from a research project carried out in an Australian university.

The scholarly teacher

A project carried out by Trigwell *et al.* (2000) in an Australian university involving both academic staff members who had recently pursued and completed a Teaching and Learning CPD programme and academic staff who had not done so, posing the question 'What do you think the scholarship of teaching is?' determined five categories of approach to the scholarship of teaching as summarised below:

A   The scholarship of teaching is about knowing the literature on teaching by collecting and reading that literature.

B   Scholarship of teaching is about improving teaching by collecting and reading the literature on teaching.

C   Scholarship of teaching is about improving student learning by investigating the learning of one's own students and one's own teaching.

D   Scholarship of teaching is about improving one's own students' learning by knowing and relating the literature on teaching and learning to discipline specific literature and knowledge.

E   The scholarship of teaching is about improving student learning within the discipline generally, by collecting and communicating results of one's own work on teaching and learning within the discipline.

(Trigwell *et al.* 2000: 159)

What is fascinating about these outcomes of the study is the ascending scale of approaches to scholarship which mirror the notions of surface and deep approaches to learning (Ramsden 2003) and which also reflect a scale of understanding of the conceptual shift from the role of teacher (as transmitter of information) to the role of facilitator of student learning, contextualised within the discipline (Stefani and Nicol 1996).

While the Australian study was small in scale it is nevertheless indicative of a positive shift in understandings of scholarship. The challenge now for universities is to promote scholarship by providing appropriate opportunities for academic staff to develop their approaches to the scholarship of learning and teaching, through action, reflection and evaluation of their current practice.

In this aspect of the agenda, universities within the UK in particular are being assisted by the increasing number and variety of development opportunities relating to teaching and learning available to academic staff. This is a further positive indication of the increasing attention being paid to the quality of the student learning experience within higher education.

In the previous chapter, Liz Beaty gives a very detailed account of the history of the genesis of many of the highly significant 'development organisations' which have promoted a scholarly approach to learning and teaching. The following section of this chapter will summarise the significance of the most recent of these developmental organisations to the promotion of the scholarship of teaching.

Promoting the scholarship of teaching and learning

Within the UK, as mentioned above, it has become increasingly common for new faculty members to be encouraged to pursue a professional qualification relating to teaching and learning. Many of these professional qualification CPD programmes were initially accredited by SEDA (Staff and Educational Development Association, UK) whose mission as a professional association is to improve all aspects of learning, teaching and training in higher education through staff and educational development (SEDA 2002). SEDA accreditation of professional CPD programmes required them to promote a deep knowledge and understanding of teaching and academic practice and to encourage in course participants a commitment to a set of values that underpin good practice. Furthermore, the Dearing Report (NCIHE 1997a) recommended the professionalisation of teaching in higher education, and that a formal institute should be set up to accredit the practice of university teachers. This recommendation resulted in the setting up in 1999 of the Institute for Learning and Teaching in Higher Education (ILTHE). The ILTHE was launched with the support of government and all major higher education stakeholders, and has recently been re-launched as the Higher Education Academy (HEA).

The ILTHE was a membership organisation open to everyone engaged in teaching and learning support in higher education. Its aims were to enhance the status of teaching, improve the experience of learning, and support innovation in higher education teaching and learning. One of its key roles was to accredit the practice of individual staff members and to accredit postgraduate programmes of initial professional development.

The purpose of the ILTHE, as it was initially set up, fitted neatly with Boyer's notion of the scholarship of teaching as encompassing initial preparation for teaching in higher education, encouraging staff to pursue appropriate continuing professional development and to provide evidence of their scholarship. The work of the ILTHE encouraged the development of rigorous postgraduate programmes encompassing all aspects of teaching, learning and assessment, course and curriculum design, development and delivery.

The growth in postgraduate accredited programmes on teaching and learning is further contributing to the current promotion of the scholarship of teaching (Gordon et al. 2001), encouraging academic staff to put more emphasis on understanding disciplinary based pedagogy and viewing teaching and learning as legitimate researchable activities. The provision of such accredited courses and programmes has now become a major aspect of the work of staff and educational development units. While it is not yet the case that all postgraduate programmes on offer place an emphasis on research and scholarship, Stefani and Elton (2002) suggest that it must be one of the main features of any really successful programme of CPD for academic teachers to convince them that university teaching is a problematic and researchable activity.

While the setting up of the ILTHE was unique to the UK, it is clear from the growing body of pedagogical research that many universities in Canada, Australia and New Zealand for example are in the process of establishing postgraduate programmes relating to academic practice, and new faculty are encouraged to pursue such programmes. Recent information from the Australian Universities Teaching Committee indicates that a National Institute for Learning and Teaching in Higher Education will be established as part of a strategy to promote excellence in learning and teaching. The Australian Institute will be established as a national focus for the enhancement of learning and teaching in Australian higher education institutions. It is very likely that the scholarship of teaching will be high on the agenda of this new institute.

A further indication of the growing importance of teaching and learning and acknowledgement of the fidelity of the discipline was the setting up within the UK of the Learning and Teaching Subject Network (LTSN), funded by HEFCE and now part of the HEA. The LTSN was set up specifically to provide resources 'tailor made' to the teaching and learning demands of 24 different disciplinary based subject areas, and for the purposes of disseminating good practice within and across different subject areas (Allan 2000). This was an explicit signal that pedagogical development could and arguably should occur within the disciplinary base. It was also a response to the difficulties of expecting staff to transfer their learning from generic workshops on issues relating to teaching and learning, into their disciplinary base where they may be trying to effect change as a 'lone ranger'. The existence of the subject networks allows for staff from any discipline to share and explore scholarship with like-minded colleagues.

The overall objectives of the new HEA, launched in Autumn 2004, are to promote higher education by:

- providing strategic advice to the higher education sector, government, funding bodies and others on policies designed to enhance the student experience;
- supporting curriculum and pedagogical development across the whole spectrum of higher education activity;
- facilitating the professional development of all staff in higher education.

The overall concept of the 'Academy' is tangible evidence of a serious attempt to further promote a reflective and scholarly approach to teaching in higher education today and it is likely that developments that are promoted in one country will disseminate more globally.

Concluding remarks

Despite the growing recognition of the importance of taking a more scholarly approach to teaching, higher education institutions still face many challenges in promoting scholarship across the institution. While postgraduate accredited programmes relating to teaching are primarily targeted at new faculty members, there is a difficulty in encouraging more experienced staff to continuously reflect on and develop their approaches to teaching. While the HEA currently provides different routes to membership for experienced faculty, the challenge is to provide ongoing, appropriate opportunities to engage in the scholarship of teaching.

At institutional level, however, there are a number of approaches that could be taken to build capacity for the scholarship of teaching. There is, for example, a general need for institutions to identify and raise awareness of the opportunities available to staff to engage in pedagogical research and development. There is a need to identify gaps in current provision of academic staff development with regard to pedagogical development, and an urgent need, as Laurillard and McConnell argue in their chapters, to ensure that increased use of ICT in teaching is underpinned by pedagogical knowledge and understanding.

It is highly unlikely that an ethos of scholarship as relating to learning and teaching can be promoted at an institutional level without clear and explicit support from senior managers. Strenuous efforts must therefore be made to provide different career pathways for faculty and to ensure that fair promotion and advancement strategies exist that include the scholarship of teaching as a key criterion.

Institutions must decide what action should be taken and by whom, to support and promote scholarship across the institution. Pursuing a more scholarly and reflective approach to classroom practice should not be considered merely as an optional extra, pursued by enthusiasts.

Finally, higher education institutions must actively promote scholarship through the development of better 'impact evaluation tools' such that examples of staff development policies that encourage an integrated approach to the development of the teacher/researcher in higher education and support the scholarship of teaching can be highlighted, disseminated and encouraged.

Conclusions

Chapter 10

Interpreting the developments

Possible futures for learning and teaching in higher education

Paul Ashwin

The previous chapters of this book have examined the development of learning, learning technologies and teaching in higher education. In examining these developments, they have also identified a number of tensions both in the ways that learning and teaching have developed in the past, and in the forces that will shape them in the future. The purpose of this concluding chapter is to draw together the insights from these chapters and to consider what they might suggest collectively for the future development of learning and teaching in higher education. My focus, then, is on connecting the ideas from the earlier chapters rather than considering them in the context of the literature on, or recent trends in, the development of learning and teaching in higher education. My reason for taking this approach is to try to make the tensions in these chapters explicit by exploring the different futures that they suggest and to use these to construct a set of questions that can be used to critically examine the future development of learning and teaching in higher education. This approach has two implications that are worth noting. First, it means that knowledge of the arguments contained in the previous chapters is assumed in this chapter. Second, it means that this chapter has more of a discursive focus and, as such, makes very few references beyond what is contained in the previous chapters of this book.

The first part of this chapter, then, briefly outlines the developments in learning, learning technologies and teaching that have been discussed in the previous chapters. I then focus on the tensions in these developments through the device of constructing two possible futures for learning and teaching in higher education. These futures are not intended to offer an accurate prediction of the future but are instead intended to explore and extend the logic of different ways of thinking about the development of learning and teaching. Finally, I use the differences between these two futures to argue for a more critical approach to the development of learning and teaching in higher education.

What changes have we seen in learning and teaching in higher education?

There are many changes that have been described throughout this book. Indeed, they seem to underline how huge the extent of change in the development of learning and teaching in higher education has been over the last 30 years.

In terms of the development of learning, there has been a shift in the way that learning and teaching interactions have been thought about. Boud's chapter shows how there have been shifts in the theories underpinning learning and teaching innovations from the behaviourism prominent in the early 1970s to more recent ideas developed from constructivism and post-modernism. Equally, the appropriate authority of teachers in higher education has increasingly become the focus of discussion, as Hodgson shows in her chapter examining more participative forms of assessment that seek to give students more say in the grading of their work. Denicolo's chapter examines changes in the way that research degrees have been thought about, from a focus on doctorates as a preparation to become an academic researcher to doctorates being thought about in terms of preparing students to undertake a number of roles in society and the resulting rethinking of the support of these students. Bridge's chapter discusses changes in the position of non-traditional students in higher education from making up a small number of students in the early 1970s to becoming an increasingly important part of higher education, in terms of both the number of students who can be considered to be 'non-traditional' and the changes that non-traditional students have precipitated in the ways that the learning of all students has been supported.

In learning technologies, Laurillard's chapter charts the unprecedented shift in the technology available to support learning from the interactive computers that were just beginning to come into universities in the 1970s to the hand-held portable technology that is offered in the form of 3G mobile phones, whilst McConnell's chapter outlines the shifts in the focus of technology from the individual to more cooperative forms of learning that attempt to provide a strong sense of community.

In the development of teaching, Beaty's chapter charts how teaching in higher education is increasingly becoming a professional activity operating within professional standards. Stefani's chapter shows how this is equally being thought about as a more scholarly process in terms of both the teaching that is offered to students and the educational development that is used to support teaching staff.

This way of summarising the developments in learning, learning technologies and teaching, whilst providing a useful overview, has one major disadvantage. This is that it appears to suggest that the developments described were almost inevitable and were characterised by smooth transitions from one approach to learning and teaching to another. However, as the earlier chapters demonstrate, these changes were beset by tensions. It is these tensions that are the focus of the next section.

Two futures for the development of learning and teaching in higher education

In order to bring together and explore the tensions in the development of learning and teaching that have been examined in the previous chapters, I have constructed two possible futures for the development of learning and teaching in higher education. One, a bleak future, is characterised by alienation and separation, and the other, a bright future, is characterised by engagement and integration (see Mann 2001 for an excellent exploration of alienation, engagement and the student experience).

The bleak future of learning and teaching in higher education

There is a bleak future for learning and teaching in higher education. As more and more students enter into higher education, the infrastructure will become more stretched than ever before. Discourses of 'learner-centredness' and 'learner autonomy' will increasingly be used to justify the limited resources available, as, more and more, undergraduate and taught postgraduate students are expected to learn on their own. Learning technologies will become increasingly important in these students' learning, with the internet and subject databases acting as the key sources of information for students. This information will be largely presented in the form of text, which students will access whilst working on their own. As a result students will feel increasingly isolated and alienated from their fellow students and teachers. This sense of alienation will be clearest in assessment practices, in which students will have judgements of their work given by their tutors but will have little understanding of the basis of these judgements or the ways in which they might improve their work.

PhD programmes will become increasingly driven by completion rates and the need to maintain external funding. There will be many more students studying for many different forms of PhDs but their experience will be of mass-produced qualifications that force them to jump through a number of skills hoops without really asking them to engage deeply with their research. These skills will only need to be demonstrated once and then will be instantly forgotten, and even if remembered students will have no sense of how they might apply them outside the context of academia. These students will have so much to do in their time-limited three years (or part-time equivalent) that rather than following their research interests, they will feel forced to stick to the safe and well-trodden research paths that others have taken before them.

Support for teaching will be very different in different types of institutions. In the old research-led universities, almost all undergraduate teaching will be carried out by postgraduate students, whilst academics focus on their research. In the new universities, all academics will be expected to focus on their teaching. This will mean that academics in these different types of institutions will be assessed by different criteria. Those in the old universities will be judged according to their research and those in new universities by their teaching. The professional teaching standards that are introduced will have been forced on the profession and will enforce the same model of professional practice onto all teachers, whether they are postgraduate research students in old universities or established academics in new universities. They will encourage teaching that is unscholarly, focused on a 'what works' approach that pays no attention to the disciplinary and institutional context of learning and teaching. This teaching will be supported by unscholarly academic developers, who are imposed on unwilling teachers and postgraduates to enact the ever-changing visions of vice-chancellors and government ministers.

To summarise, this bleak future will be one of isolation and alienation. Students will feel isolated and alienated from their teachers, their educational institutions and the disciplines they are attempting to study. Teaching and research will be isolated from each other physically, with the two activities taking place in different institutions or parts of a single institution, and with different members of staff engaged in each activity. Those who act as teachers will feel hostile to the academic developers who seek to support their work, as the focus is increasingly upon their performance as teachers rather than the learning environment that they establish with their students.

The bright future of learning and teaching in higher education

There is a bright future for learning and teaching in higher education. In the next 30 years, learning and teaching will become more learner-centred. Students will increasingly participate in the assessment of their work, through constructive dialogue with other students and their teachers. Learning and teaching will increasingly be seen as integrated activities, with students and teachers learning and teaching together in collaborative learning environments. Learning technologies will play a key role in supporting these environments, as learning packages are developed that involve students in developing their creativity through interactive transactions with other learners rather than simply accessing texts. Simulations will strengthen students' engagement with the scholarly texts of their disciplines, as they allow them to experience the meaning of the key concepts through engagement with other learners. This technology will also be focused on communities of learners, with a primary position given to collaboration and the development of shared understandings. Participation in these learning communities will develop a strong sense of shared ownership of the knowledge that is developed within higher education.

This will increase students' sense of involvement in their academic institutions at all levels of higher education. PhD supervision will become increasingly collegial as supervisors and students interact as near peers, with students having far greater choice in the way they research their area of interest. Genuinely interdisciplinary research will become the norm rather than the exception. There will be an increased integration of knowledge and skills that are assessed as a whole in the final thesis, rather than as a set of discrete skills.

The development of teaching standards across higher education will create an identity of academic-as-teacher–researcher across the sector with equal weight and reward being given to both activities, and academics free to specialise in either or both and to change their specialism throughout their careers. These scholarly teachers will be supported by scholarly educational developers and together they will investigate learning and teaching contexts to design curricula that make best use of the face-to-face and online environments and involve students in the assessment of their work.

To summarise, this bright future will be one of integration and critical engagement. Students will feel critically engaged by their teachers and their disciplines and will feel a part of the institutions in which they are studying. Teaching and research will be integrated together, with academics involving their students in aspects of their research and students' learning characterised by the same processes of discovery as the research of their teachers. These teacher–researchers will work in integrated teams with academic developers and, together with students, they will develop learning environments in which learning and teaching are mutually owned by all of those who are part of the learning and teaching process.

Towards a critical future for the development of learning and teaching in higher education

As I indicated earlier, the bleak and the bright futures described above are intended to draw out the tensions in the forces that will shape learning and teaching in the future that were outlined in the earlier chapters of this book. In one future, forces that seek to isolate learning and teaching from the other activities of universities dominate, and the learning and teaching process is seen in simple terms and is largely viewed as the transfer of information. This has the effect of alienating both teachers and students from the learning and teaching process. In the other future, forces that seek to integrate learning and teaching with other activities hold sway. In this future, the learning and teaching process is viewed as complex and the focus is on providing a learning environment that will enable students and teachers to engage in understanding their disciplines in a mutually enriching process.

We now move to the thornier subject of what might be done to encourage engagement and integration in learning and teaching in higher education. Based on the analyses offered by the contributors to this book, I argue that what is needed is a more critical approach to the development of learning and teaching in higher education. As a contribution to this future, I outline four key questions that can be used to critically examine the future development of learning, learning technologies and teaching in higher education.

Before setting out these questions, it should be noted that I do not claim that they, or the futures I have described above, are wholly original. Rather, my claim is that they are the key lessons that have emerged from the review of the development of learning and teaching in higher education that has been undertaken in this book. Given this, they have a slightly different emphasis and form than those that have been raised in previous and current debates around learning and teaching in higher education.

Question 1: What are the values and purposes underlying models of learning and teaching in higher education?

One of the key issues emerging from a number of chapters (in particular those of Boud and Laurillard) is the importance of focusing on the values and purposes of learning and teaching in higher education. This is a contested terrain and one in which it is important for all of those who have a stake in learning and teaching in higher education to debate. The position that has emerged through this book is that the purpose of learning and teaching in higher education is for students and academics to engage together critically in coming to know the disciplines and knowledge that make up higher education. This was a clear difference between the bright and bleak futures of learning and teaching in higher education. In the bleak future, the purposes of learning and teaching in higher education are vague and seem only to be directed towards academics preparing students for future activities, such as employment. Whereas in the bright future the purpose is clear. It is about students becoming critically engaged with their tutors and disciplines and through this engagement developing a shared ownership of the knowledge that they are recreating through their academic studies. This critical engagement will undoubtedly prepare students for the future, indeed, as Bowden and Marton (1998) argue, it will more importantly prepare students for a future that is unknowable.

Question 2: Is learning and teaching being presented as a collective or individual activity?

Another related issue that was focused on in Boud's and McConnell's chapters was the importance of focusing on learning and teaching communities rather than simply on individual learners. In the bleak future, we saw how students were isolated from their teachers and other students as learning and teaching were viewed as individual processes. The bright future instead was categorised by students learning together in collaborative environments. Such learning and teaching communities include both teachers and students and, as Denicolo argued in her chapter, can reach their most collegial form in doctoral work.

Such learning and teaching communities recognise individual students and teachers but they also recognise that such individuals are part of a wider learning and teaching context. As has been shown in every chapter in this book, the learning and teaching context has a key role in shaping students' and teachers' experiences of learning and teaching in higher education. Thus it is vital that they are considered in relation to this environment. Thinking about learning and teaching communities rather than individual learners is an important way of doing this. A focus at the level of individual students and teachers is problematic for two reasons. First, when thinking about learning, it encourages students to think about how they respond to the environment that is established by their teachers rather than thinking about how they contribute to that environment. Second, it suggests that individual teachers and students are solely responsible for creating that environment rather than suggesting that such environments are also partly created by the institutions and departments in which learning and teaching interactions take place.

Question 3: How are power relations thought about in learning and teaching in higher education?

An issue that is often raised when thinking about the issues discussed under Question 2 is that of power relations within learning and teaching communities. Often the notion of collaboration within a learning and teaching community can obscure the power relations that exist between students, teachers and their institutions. Question 3 draws attention to the issue of power that was raised in a number of the chapters in this book. What is clear from these chapters is that power relations need to be questioned in order for learning and teaching in higher education to remain consistent with its critical nature outlined under Question 1. For example, as Hodgson emphasises, we should question why students commonly have such a passive role in the assessment of their work. Equally, as Beaty emphasises, we need to question the ways in which teaching standards are introduced into higher education, and examine how power operates in the introduction of such standards.

In the bleak and bright futures described above, there were clear differences in the ways that power operated and was thought about. In the bleak future, power was something that was enforced from above, leaving students and teachers in a position where they either went along with the system or were forced to demonstrate their resistance by refusing to engage with it. In the bright future, power was viewed as being held by all of those involved in the learning and teaching process and decisions were reached through negotiation. This difference was perhaps clearest in the two different models of academic development in the two futures. In the bleak future, academic development was focused on achieving the aims of vice-chancellors whilst in the bright future it was about developers and teachers working together to come to new understandings of the learning and teaching situations in a way that was much closer to the notion of the scholarship of academic development that is examined in Stefani's chapter.

Question 4: What models of change are being used in developing learning and teaching in higher education?

This final question is related to each of the other questions. It is related to the first question, which emphasised the importance of thinking about the values and purposes of higher education. If learning and teaching in higher education are about critical engagement, then it would seem appropriate that the models of change that are employed in their development are thought about critically. It is related to the second question, in that models of change need to be focused at a community rather than an individual level. It is related to the third question, in that issues of power are vital in the change process.

As Laurillard and Bridge argue, uncritical, individualistic, top-down methods of introducing change are inappropriate for introducing successful innovation into higher education. Laurillard argues for cybernetic models that allow for two-way communication, are based on networks rather than individuals, and are focused on negotiation and local dialogues, which encourage local versions of innovations to develop. Such models of change allow students, academics, support staff and managers to critically engage with any changes introduced and to develop them based on their knowledge of local conditions. This is crucial in preventing alienation within the learning and teaching process. The more models of learning and teaching are enforced on students and staff, the more they will be rejected or result in simple compliance.

Concluding remarks

Whilst the direction of the future development of learning and teaching in higher education is uncertain, consideration of the above questions should at least provide a framework with which to engage critically with these changes, to question their assumptions and to ask how they will affect the quality of student and teacher engagement in learning and teaching in higher education.

In Chapter 1, I argued that this book was held together by two commitments. First, the commitment to start with the learner, be they student or teacher, when thinking about ways of developing learning and teaching in higher education, and second, the commitment to making sense of past changes in learning and teaching in higher education in order to offer an insight into how they might be developed in the future. I hope that this book has suggested, on the basis of such commitments, some ways in which to develop a more critical understanding of the development of learning and teaching in higher education.

References

Acker, S. (1999) 'Students and supervisors, the ambiguous relationship, perspectives on the supervisory process in Britain and Canada', in Holbrook, A. and Johnson, S. (eds) *Supervision of Postgraduate Research in Education*, Victoria, Australia, Australian Association for Research in Education.

Alexander, S. and McKenzie, J. (1998) *An Evaluation of Information Technology Projects for University Learning: Executive Summary*, http://www.dest.gov.au/archive/cutsd/publications/exsummary.html, last accessed 25 January 2005.

Allan, C. (2000) 'The Learning and Teaching Support Network (LTSN): the implications for educational developers', *Educational Developments*, 1 (2): 1–3.

Anderson, G. and Boud, D. (1996) 'Introducing learning contracts: a flexible way to learn', *Innovations in Education and Training International*, 33: 221–7.

Anderson, G., Boud, D. and Sampson, J. (1996) *Learning Contracts: A Practical Guide*, London, Kogan Page.

Anderson, G., Boud, D. and Sampson, J. (1998) 'Qualities of learning contracts', in Stephenson, J. and Yorke, M. (eds) *Capability and Quality in Higher Education*, London, Kogan Page.

Asensio, M., Hodgson, V. and Trehan, K. (2000) 'Is there a difference? Contrasting experiences of face to face and online learning', in Asensio, M., Foster, J., Hodgson, V. and McConnell, D. (eds) (2000) *Networked Learning 2000, Innovative Approaches to Lifelong Learning and Higher Education Through the Internet*, Sheffield, University of Sheffield.

Ashwell, N. (2003) 'Perceptions of inter-agency collaboration', unpublished PhD thesis, University of Reading.

Ashworth, P. (2004) 'Developing useable pedagogic research skills', in Rust C. (ed.) *Improving Student Learning: Theory Research and Scholarship*, Oxford, Oxford Centre for Staff and Learning Development.

Asmar, C. (1999) 'Scholarship, experience or both?: A developer's approach to cross-cultural teaching', *International Journal of Academic Development*, 4 (1): 18–27.

Axelrod, R. (1990) *The Evolution of Cooperation*, London, Penguin Books.

Banks, S., Lally, V. and McConnell, D. (eds) (2002) *Collaborative E-Learning in Higher Education: Issues and Strategies*, Sheffield, School of Education, University of Sheffield.

Banks, S., Goodyear, P., Hodgson, V. and McConnell, D. (2003) 'Introduction to the special issue on advances in research on networked learning', *Instructional Science*, 31: 1–6.

Barajas, M. and Owen, M. (2000) 'Implementing virtual learning environments: looking for a holistic approach', *Educational Technology and Society*, 3 (3): 39–53.

Barnett, R. (1997) *Higher Education: A Critical Business*, Buckingham, The Society for Research into Higher Education and Open University Press.

Baume, D. and Baume, C. (1996) 'A national scheme to accredit university teachers', *International Journal for Academic Development*, 1 (2): 51–8.

Beard, R. (1968) *Research into Teaching Methods: Mainly in British Universities*, Second Edition, London, The Society for Research into Higher Education.

Beard, R. (1970) *Teaching and Learning in Higher Education*, Harmondsworth, Penguin.

Beaty, L. (1995) 'Working across the hierarchy', in Brew, A. (ed.) *Directions in Staff Development*, Buckingham, The Society for Research into Higher Education and Open University Press.

Beaty, L., Hodgson, V., Mann, S. and McConnell, D. (Convenors) (2002) *Manifesto: Towards E-Quality in Networked E-Learning in Higher Education*, http://www.csalt.lancs.ac.uk/esrc/manifesto.htm, accessed May 2002.

Becher, T. and Trowler, P. (2001) *Academic Tribes and Territories*, Second Edition, Buckingham, The Society for Research in Higher Education and Open University Press.

Becher, T., Henkel, M. and Kogan, M. (1994) *Graduate Education in Britain*, London, Jessica Kingsley.

Becker, H., Geer, B. and Hughes, E. (1968) *Making the Grade: The Academic Side of Academic Life*, New York, John Wiley.

Bentley, T. and Wilsdon, J. (2003) *The Adaptive State*, London, Demos.

Biggs, J. (1978) 'Individual and group differences in study processes', *British Journal of Educational Psychology*, 48: 266–79.

Biggs, J. (1999) *Teaching for Quality Learning at University: What the Student Does*, Buckingham, The Society for Research in Higher Education and Open University Press.

Black, T., Hill, E. and Acker, S. (1994) 'Thesis supervision in the social sciences, managed or negotiated?', *Higher Education*, 28 (4): 483–98.

Bligh, J. (1971) *What's the Use of Lectures?*, London, University Teaching Methods Unit, University of London.

Boot, R. and Hodgson, V. (1987) 'Open learning, meaning and experience', in Hodgson, V., Mann, S. and Snell, R. (eds) *Beyond Distance Teaching: Towards Open Learning*, Buckingham, The Society for Research into Higher Education and Open University Press.

Boud, D. (ed.) (1985) *Problem-Based Learning in Education for the Professions*, Sydney, Higher Education Research and Development Society of Australasia.

Boud, D. (1986) 'Implementing student self assessment', *Higher Education Research and Development*, 5: 3–10.

Boud, D. (1987) 'A facilitator's view of adult learning', in Boud, D. and Griffin, V. (eds) *Appreciating Adults Learning: From the Learner's Perspective*, London, Kogan Page.

Boud, D. (1995) *Enhancing Learning through Self Assessment*, London, Kogan Page.

Boud, D. (1998) 'How can university work-based courses contribute to lifelong learning?', in Holford, J., Jarvis, P. and Griffin, C. (eds) *International Perspectives on Lifelong Learning*, London, Kogan Page.

Boud, D. and Feletti, G. (1997) 'Changing problem-based learning', in Boud, D. and Feletti, G. (eds) *The Challenge of Problem-Based Learning*, Second, Revised Edition, London, Kogan Page.

Boud, D., Bridge, W. A. and Willoughby, L. (1975) 'PSI now: a review of progress and problems', *British Journal of Educational Technology*, 6 (2):15–34.

Boud, D., Solomon, N. and Symes, C. (2001) 'New practices for new times', in Boud, D. and Solomon, N. (eds) *Work-Based Learning: A New Higher Education?* Buckingham, The Society for Research into Higher Education and Open University Press.

Bourdieu, P. (1990) *Homo Academicus*, Cambridge, Polity.

Bowden, J. and Marton, F. (1998) *The University of Learning: Beyond Quality and Competence in Higher Education*, London, Kogan Page.

Boyer Commission on Educating Undergraduates in the Research University (1998) *Re-Inventing Undergraduate Education: A Blueprint for America's Research Universities*, http://naples.cc.sunysb.edu/Press/boyer.nsf, accessed August 2004.

Boyer, E. (1990) *Scholarship Reconsidered: Priorities of the Professoriate*, New Jersey, Carnegie Foundation for the Advancement of Teaching.

Brabdon, D. and Hollingshead, A. (1999) 'Collaborative learning and computer-supported groups', *Communication Education*, 48 (2): 108–25.

Breivik, P. (1998) *Student Learning in the Information Age*, American Council on Education, Oryx Press.

Brew, A. (2001) *The Nature of Research: Inquiry in Academic Contexts*, London, RoutledgeFalmer.

Bringelson, L. and Carey, T. (2000) 'Different keystrokes for different folks: designing online venues for professional communities', *Educational Technology and Society*, 3 (3): 58–64.

Brookfield, S. (2001) 'Unmasking power, Foucault and adult learning', *Canadian Journal for the Study of Adult Education*, 15 (1): 1–23.

Brush, T. (1997) 'The effects of group composition on achievement and time on task for students completing ILS activities in cooperative pairs', *Journal of Research on Computing in Education*, 30 (1): 2–17.

Burgess, R. (1996) 'Trends and developments in postgraduate education and training in the UK', *Journal of Education Policy*, 11 (1): 125–32.

Burgess, R. (ed.) (1997) *Beyond the First Degree: Graduate Education, Lifelong Learners and Careers*, Buckingham, The Society for Research into Higher Education and Open University Press.

Cameron, I. (2004) Keynote presentation, Roberts Policy Forum, UK GRAD, Manchester, January.

Carnegie Academy for Scholarship in Teaching and Learning (CASTL) (2000) *Information Programme Booklet*, Menlo Park, California, Carnegie Foundation for the Advancement of Teaching.

Clandinin, D. and Connelly, F. (2000) *Narrative Inquiry: Experience and Story in Qualitative Research*, San Francisco, Jossey-Bass Publishers.

Clark, J. (1981) *Educational Development*, London, Kogan Page.

Clegg, S. and Gall, I. (1998) 'The discourse of research degree supervision: a case study of supervisor training', *Higher Education Research and Development* 17 (3): 323–32.

Clegg, S., Tan, J. and Saeidi, S. (2002) 'Reflecting or acting? Reflective practice and continuing professional development in UK higher education', *Reflective Practice*, 3 (1): 131–46.

Collis, B. (1998) 'WWW-based environments for collaborative group work', *Education and Information Technology*, 3: 231–45.

Collis, B. and van der Wende, M. (eds) (2002) *Models of Technology and Change in Higher Education*, http://www.utwente.nl/cheps/documenten/ictrapport.pdf, accessed January 2003.

Commission of the European Communities (2000) *Designing Tomorrow's Education*, Brussels, Communication from the Commission to the Council and the European Parliament.

Commission of the European Communities (2003) *Researchers in the European Research Area: One Profession, Multiple Careers*, Brussels, Communication from the Commission to the Council and the European Parliament.

Committee on Higher Education (1963) *Higher Education* (Robbins Report), London, HMSO.

Committee of Inquiry into the Education of Children from Ethnic Minority Groups (1981) *West Indian Children in our Schools: Interim Report of the Committee of Inquiry into the Education of Children from Ethnic Minority Groups* (Rampton Report), London, HMSO.

Coopers and Lybrand, Institute of Education, and Tavistock Institute (1996) 'Evaluation of the Teaching and Learning Technology Programme (TLTP): executive summary', *Active Learning*, 5: 60–3.

Cowan, J. (1998) *On Becoming an Innovative University Teacher: Reflection in Action*, Buckingham, The Society for Research into Higher Education and Open University Press.

Creagh, I. and Graves, H. (2003) 'Recent trends in higher education public policy in Australia and the UK', *Perspectives*, 7 (2): 48–53.

Cryer, P. and Mertens, P. (2002) 'The PhD examination, support and training for supervisors and examiners', paper presented at The Society for Research into Higher Education Postgraduate Issues Network, March.

Darling-Hammond, L., and Snyder, J. (2000) 'Authentic assessment of teaching in context', *Teaching and Teacher Education*, 16: 523–45.

Dart, B. and Clarke, J. (1991) 'Helping students become better learners, a case study in teacher education', *Higher Education*, 22: 317–35.

Deem, R. and Brehony, K. (2000) 'Doctoral students' access to research cultures, are some more unequal than others?', *Studies in Higher Education*, 25: 150–65.

Delamont, S., Atkinson, P. and Parry, O. (2000) *The Doctoral Experience: Success and Failure in Graduate School*, London, Falmer.

Denicolo, P. (1998) 'Transforming teaching and learning in higher education', *Research and Development in Higher Education*, 21: 1–14.

Denicolo, P. (2003) 'Assessing the PhD, a constructive view of criteria', *Quality Assurance in Education*, 11 (2): 84–91.

Denicolo, P. (in press) 'Doctoral supervision of colleagues: peeling off the veneer of satisfaction and competence', *Studies in Higher Education*.

Denicolo, P. and Pope, M. (1999) 'Supervision and the overseas student', in Ryan, Y. and Zuber-Skerritt, O. (eds) *Supervising Postgraduates from Non-English Speaking Backgrounds*, Buckingham, Open University Press.

Denicolo, P., Boulter, C. and Fuller, M. (1999) 'Triangulated reflections on the examining of higher degrees: opening Pandora's box', paper presented at The International Study Association for Teachers and Teaching (ISATT) Conference, Dublin, 27–31 July.

Department for Education and Skills (DfES) (2003a) *The Future of Higher Education*, London, HMSO.

Department for Education and Skills (DfES) (2003b) *Towards a Unified E-Learning Strategy: Consultation Document* (DfES reference number DfES/0424/2003), London, DfES.

Department of Education and Science (DES) (1975) *Statistics of Education: Volume 3 Further Education*, London, HMSO.

Dillenbourg, P. (1999) 'Introduction: what do you mean by "collaborative learning"?', in Dillenbourg, P. (ed.) *Collaborative Learning: Cognitive and Computational Approaches*, Oxford, Pergamon/Elsevier Science Ltd.

Dillenbourg, P., Baker, M., Blaye, A. and O'Malley, C. (1996) 'The evolution of research on collaborative learning', in Spada, E. and Reiman, P. (eds) *Learning in Humans and Machine: Towards an Interdisciplinary Learning Science*, Oxford, Elsevier.

Donaldson, F. (1994) *British Council: The First 50 years*, London, Jonathan Cape.

Dugdale, K. (1997) 'Mass higher education, mass graduate employment in the 1990s', in Burgess R. (ed.) *Beyond the First Degree, Graduate Education, Lifelong Learners and Careers*, Buckingham, The Society for Research in Higher Education and Open University Press.

Duisburg, M. and Hoope, U. (1999) 'Computer supported interaction analysis of group problem solving', in *Proceedings of the Conference on Computer Supported Collaborative Learning*, CSCL, 9: 398–405. Palo Alto, CA, December.

Duke, C (1997) 'Lifelong, post experience, postgraduate, symphony or dichotomy', in Burgess R. (ed.) *Beyond the First Degree, Graduate Education, Lifelong Learners and Careers*, Buckingham, The Society for Research in Higher Education and Open University Press.

Economic and Social Research Council (ESRC) (2000) *Postgraduate Training Guidelines*, Swindon, Economic and Social Research Council.

Eggins, H. and MacDonald, R. (eds) *The Scholarship of Academic Development*, Buckingham, The Society for Research in Higher Education and Open University Press.

Elton, L. (1973) 'Instructional methods in university science education', in Billing, D. and Furniss, B. (eds) *Aims, Methods and Assessment in Advanced Science Education*, London, Heydon.

Elton, L. (1977) 'Innovation and the role of educational media', in Beug, J. (ed.) *Innovation in Teaching and Learning in Higher Education*, Dublin, Higher Education Authority.

Elton, L. (1992) 'Research, teaching and scholarship in an expanding higher education system', *Higher Education Quarterly*, 46: 252–67.

Elton, L. (1995) 'An institutional framework', in Brew, A. (ed.) *Directions in Staff Development*, Buckingham, The Society for Research in Higher Education and Open University Press.

Elton, L. (1999) 'New ways of learning in higher education: managing the change', *Tertiary Education and Management*, 5: 207–25.

Elton, L. (2000) 'The UK Research Assessment Exercise: unintended consequences', *Higher Education Quarterly*, 54: 274–83.

Elton, L. (2001) 'Research and teaching: conditions for a positive link', *Teaching in Higher Education*, 6 (1): 43–56.

Elton, L. (2003) *Seven Pillars of Assessment Wisdom*, http://www.ltsn.ac.uk, accessed August 2004.

Elton, L. and Laurillard, D. (1979) 'Trends in research on student learning', *Studies in Higher Education*, 4: 87–102.

Elton L. and Pope, M. (1989) 'Research supervision, the value of collegiality', *Cambridge Journal of Education*, 19 (3): 267–75.

Elton, L. and Cryer, P. (1994) 'Quality and change in higher education', *Innovative Higher Education*, 18: 205–20.

Elton, L. and Johnston, B. (2002) *Assessment in Universities: A Critical Review of Research*, http://www.ltsn.ac.uk/application.asp?section=generic&app=resources. asp&process=full_record&id=13, accessed August 2004.

Elton, L., Boud, D., Nuttall, J. and Stace, B. (1973) 'Teach yourself paradigm: the Keller Plan', *Chemistry in Britain*, 9 (4): 164–8.

Entwistle, N. and Entwistle, A. (1997) 'Revision and the experience of understanding', in Marton, F., Hounsell, D. and Entwistle, N. (eds) *The Experience of Learning*, Second Edition, Scottish Academic Press, Edinburgh.

Entwistle, N. and Wilson, J. (1977) *Degrees of Excellence: The Academic Achievement Game*, London, Hodder and Stoughton.

Entwistle, N., McCune, V. and Walker, P. (2000) 'Conceptions, styles and approaches within higher education, analytic abstractions and everyday experience', in Sternberg, R. and Zhang, L-F. (eds) *Perspectives on Thinking, Learning, and Cognitive Styles*, Mahwah, NJ, Lawrence Erlbaum.

Eraut, M. (2000) 'Non-formal learning and tacit knowledge in professional work', *Journal of Educational Psychology*, 70: 113–36.

Evans, L. and Abbot, I. (1998) *Teaching and Learning in Higher Education*, London, Cassell.

Evans, N. (2001) *The Institute for Learning and Teaching in Higher Education: Institutions, Academics and the Assessment of Prior Experiential Learning*, London, RoutledgeFalmer.

Falchikov, N. (1995) 'Peer feedback marking, developing peer assessment', *Innovations in Education and Training International*, 32 (2): 175–87.

Fallows, S. and Bhanot, R. (eds) (2002) *Educational Development through Information and Communications Technology*, London, Kogan Page.

Fazackerley, A. (2004) 'Survey: university life is a far cry from stereotype', *Times Higher Education Supplement*, 23 April.

Forsyth, A. and Furlong, A. (2002) *Losing Out?: Socioeconomic Disadvantage and Experience in Further Education*, London, Policy Press.

Foucault, M. (1979) *Discipline and Punish: The Birth of the Prison*, Hardmondsworth, Penguin.

Gellert, C. (1993) 'Academic drift and blurring of boundaries in systems of higher education', *Higher Education in Europe*, 18 (2): 78–84.

Gibbs, G., Morgan, A. and Taylor, E. (1984) 'The world of the learner', in Marton, F., Hounsell, D. and Entwistle, N. (eds) *The Experience of Learning*, Scottish Academic Press, Edinburgh.

Gibbs, G., Habeshaw, T. and Yorke, M. (2000) 'Institutional learning and teaching strategies in English higher education', *Higher Education*, 40: 351–72.

Gilchrist, R., Phillips, D. and Ross, A. (2003) 'Participation and potential participation in UK higher education', in Archer, L., Hutchings, M. and Ross, A. (eds) *Higher Education and Social Class: Issues of Exclusion and Inclusion*, London, RoutledgeFalmer.

Giroux, H. (1999) 'Cultural studies as public pedagogy: making the pedagogical more political' in Peters, M., Ghiraldelli, P., Standish, P. and Zarnic, B. (eds) *Encyclopaedia of Philosophy of Education*, http://www.vusst.hr/ENCYCLOPAEDIA/cultural_studies.htm, last accessed January 2005.

Gordon, G. (1998) 'Staff and student roles: responding to change', SRHE/THES/CVCP Seminar, University of Strathclyde.

Gordon, G., D'Andrea, V., Gosling, D. and Stefani, L. (2001) *Building Capacity for Change: Research on the Scholarship of Teaching: Review Report for the Higher Education Funding Council for England (HEFCE)*, Bristol, HEFCE.

Gore, J. M. (1995) 'Foucault's poststructuralism and observational education research: a study of power relations', in Smith, R. and Wexler, P. (eds) *After Postmodernism: Education, Politics and Identity*, London, Falmer Press.

Gosling, D. (2001) 'Educational development units in the UK: what are they doing five years on?' *International Journal of Academic Development*, 6 (1): 74–90.

Gosling, D. and D'Andrea, V. (2002) 'How educational development/learning and teaching centres help higher education institutions manage change', *Educational Developments*, 3 (2): 1–3.

Green, H. and Shaw, M. (1999) 'Continuous professional development: emerging trends in the UK', *Quality Assurance in Education*, 7: 169–76.

Habeshaw, T., Habeshaw, S. and Gibbs, G. (1989) *53 Interesting Ways to Help Your Students Study*, Bristol T.E.S.

Halsey, A. (1997) *The Decline of Donnish Dominion: The British Academic Professions in the Twentieth Century*, Oxford: Clarendon Press.

Halsey, J. and Leslie, W. (2003) *Britain's White Paper Turns Higher Education Away from the EU*, London, Centre for Higher Education Research and Information, Open University.

Hannan, A. and Silver, H. (2002) *Innovating in Higher Education: Teaching, Learning and University Culture*, Buckingham, The Society for Research in Higher Education and Open University Press.

Hanson, N. (2003) MEd Dissertation, School of Education, University of Sheffield.

Harasim, L. (1990) 'Online education: an environment for collaboration and intellectual amplification', in Harasim, L. (ed.) *Online Education: Perspectives on a New Environment*, New York, Praeger.

Harris, M. (1996) *Review of Postgraduate Education*, London, Higher Education Funding Council for England.

Hartley, J. and Fox, C. (2002) 'The viva experience, examining the examiners', *Higher Education Review*, 35 (1): 24–30.

Hayes, C. and Larson, I. (1982) *Competence and Competition*, Sheffield, Manpower Services Commission.

Heron, J. (1981) 'Self and peer assessment', in Boydell, T. and Pedlar, M. (eds) *Management Self Development: Concepts and Practices*, Farnborough, Gower.

Higher Education Funding Council for England (HEFCE) (2004) *HEFCE Strategic Plan 2003–2008* (Updated April 2004), Bristol, HEFCE.

Higher Education Funding Council for England (HEFCE) (2005) *Teaching Quality Enhancement Fund (TQEF)*, http://www.hefce.ac.uk/learning/enhance/tqef.asp, accessed January 2005.

Higher Education Statistics Agency (HESA) (2001) *Students in Higher Education Institutions 1999/2000*, Cheltenham, HESA.

Higher Education Statistics Agency (HESA) (2004) *Students in Higher Education Institutions 2002/3*, Cheltenham, HESA.

Hockey, J. (1994) 'Establishing boundaries, problems and solutions in managing PhD supervision', *Studies in Higher Education*, 16 (3): 319–71.

Hodgson, V. (2002) 'The European Union and e-learning, an examination of rhetoric, theory and practice', *Journal of Computer Assisted Learning*, 18: 240–52.

Hodgson, V. and Reynolds, M. (1987) 'The dynamics of the learning experience', in Boud, D. and Griffen, V. (eds) *Understanding Adult Learning from the Learner's Perspective*, London, Kogan Page.

Hodgson, V. and Watland, P. (2004) 'Networked learning environment designed to support a knowledge community: the learner experience', presented at the Networked Learning 2004 conference, Lancaster, April.

Hodgson, V. and Zenios, M. (2003) 'Designing networked environments to support dialogical learning', in Wasson, B., Ludvigsen, S. and Hoppe, U. (eds) *Designing for Change in Networked Learning Environments*, Dordrecht, Kluwer Academic Publishers.

Hodgson, V., Mann, S. and Snell, R. (eds) (1987) *Beyond Distance Teaching: Towards Open Learning*, Buckingham, The Society for Research in Higher Education and Open University Press.

Hogarth T., Macguire M., Pitcher J., Purcell K. and Wilson R. (1997) *The Participation of Non-Traditional Students in Higher Education*, Warwick, The University of Warwick Institute for Employment Research.

Holbrook, A. and Johnston, S. (eds) (1999) *Supervision of Postgraduate Research in Education*, Victoria, Australia, Australian Association for Research in Education.

Humphrey, R. and McCarthy, P. (1999) 'Recognising difference, providing for postgraduate students', *Studies in Higher Education*, 24: 371–85.

Huysman, M. and Gerrits, H. (1998) 'The dynamics of internet-supported team learning, a case study', in Banks, S., Graebner, C. and McConnell, D. (eds) *Networked Lifelong Learning: Innovative Approaches to Education and Training through the Internet*, Proceedings of the 1st International Conference, Sheffield, DACE, University of Sheffield.

Institute for Learning and Teaching in Higher Education (2004) *Institute for Learning and Teaching in Higher Education* http://www.ILTHE.ac.uk/, accessed August 2004.

Jenkins, A. (1996) 'Discipline-based educational development', *International Journal of Academic Development*, 1 (1): 50–62.

Jenkins, A., Breen R. and Lindsay R. (2003) *Reshaping Teaching in Higher Education: Linking Teaching with Research*, London, Kogan Page.

Jobbins, D. (2003) 'Swell Performance', *Times Higher Trends Supplement*, 19 September, i–iv.

Jonassen, D. and Kwan, H. (2001) 'Communication patterns in computer mediated versus face-to-face group problem solving', *Educational Technology, Research and Development*, 49 (1): 35–51.

Jones, C. (1998) 'Context, content and cooperation: an ethnographic study of collaborative learning online', unpublished PhD thesis, Manchester Metropolitan University, Manchester.

Jones, C. (2000) 'Understanding students' experiences of collaborative networked learning', in Asensio, M., Foster, J., Hodgson, V. and McConnell, D. (2000) *Networked Learning 2000: Innovative Approaches to Lifelong Learning and Higher Education Through the Internet*, Sheffield, University of Sheffield.

Jones, C., Turner, J. and Street B. (1999) *Students' Writing in the University*, Amsterdam/Philadelphia, John Benjamin's Publishing Company.

Kaye, A. (1992) 'Learning together apart', in Kaye, A. (ed.) *Collaborative Learning Through Computer Conferencing (The Najaden Papers)*, London, Springer.

Keisler, S. (1992) 'Talking, teaching and learning in network groups', in Kaye, A. (ed.) *Collaborative Learning through Computer Conferencing (The Najaden Papers)*, London, Springer.

Keller, F. (1968) 'Goodbye teacher ...', *Journal of Applied Behavioral Analysis*, 1: 79–98.

Klein, J. and Doran, M. (1999) 'Implementing individual and small group learning structures with a computer simulation', *Educational Technology, Research and Development*, 47 (1): 97–109.

Knowles, M. (1975) *Self-directed Learning: A Guide for Learners and Teachers*, New York, Association Press.

Knowles, M. (1978) *The Adult Learner: A Neglected Species*, Second Edition, Houston, Gulf Publishing Company.

Knowles, M. and Associates (1986) *Using Learning Contracts*, San Francisco, Jossey-Bass.

Kreber, C. and Cranton, P. (2000) 'Exploring the scholarship of teaching', *Journal of Higher Education*, 71 (4): 466–95.

Kreijns K., Kirschner P. and Jochems, W. (2002) 'The sociability of computer-supported collaborative learning environments', *Educational Technology & Society*, 5 (1): 8–22.

Laurillard, D. (1997) 'Styles and approaches in problem-solving', in Marton, F., Hounsell, D. and Entwistle, N. (eds) *The Experience of Learning*, Second Edition, Scottish Academic Press, Edinburgh.

Laurillard, D. (2002) *Rethinking University Teaching: A Conversational Framework for the Effective Use of Learning Technologies*, Second Edition, London, RoutledgeFalmer.

Lave, J. (1988) *Cognition in Practice*, Cambridge, Cambridge University Press.

Lave, J. and Wenger, E. (1991) *Situated Learning, Legitimate Peripheral Participation,* Cambridge, Cambridge University Press.

Lea, M. and Street, B. (1998) 'Student writing in higher education: an academic literacies approach', *Studies in Higher Education*, 23: 157–72.

Learning and Teaching Support Network (LTSN) (2003) *Learning and Teaching Support Network* http://www.ltsn.ac.uk/, accessed August 2004.

Learning Skills Council for England (LSC) (2002) *The Report of the Learning and Skills Council's Distributed and Electronic Learning Group*, Coventry, LSC.

Lehtinen, E., Hakkarinen, K., Lipponen, L., Rahikainen, M. and Muukkonen, H. (1999) 'Computer-supported collaborative learning: A review of research and development', in Giebers, J. (ed.) *Reports on Education*, 10, Mijmegen, Department of Educational Science, University of Mijmegen, the Netherlands.

Levy, P., Fowell, S., Bowskill, N. and Worsfold, E. (1996) 'NetLinkS, a national professional development project for networked learner support,' *Education for Information*, 14 (4): 261–78.

Lister, M., Dovey, J., Giddings, S., Grant, I. and Kelly, K. (2003) *New Media: A Critical Introduction*, London, Routledge.

Littlejohn, A. and Stefani, L. (1999) 'Effective use of technology, bridging the skills gap: a case study', *Alt-J*, 7 (2): 66–76.

Lueddeke, G. (2003) 'Professionalising teaching practice in higher education: a study of disciplinary variation and "teaching scholarship"', *Studies in Higher Education*, 28 (2): 213–28.

McConnell, D. (2000) *Implementing Computer Supported Cooperative Learning*, Second Edition, London, Kogan Page.

McConnell, D. (2002a) 'Action research and distributed problem based learning in continuing professional education', *Distance Education*, 23 (1): 59–83.

McConnell, D. (2002b) 'The experience of networked collaborative assessment', *Studies in Continuing Education*, 24 (1): 73–92.

McConnell, D (2005) 'Examining the dynamics of networked learning groups', *Studies in Higher Education*, 30 (1): 25–42.

MacDonald, R. and Wisdom, J. (eds) (2002) *Academic and Educational Development: Research, Evaluation and Changing Practice in Higher Education*, London, Kogan Page.

MacKenzie, N., Eraut, M., and Jones, H. (1970) *Teaching and Learning: An Introduction to New Methods and Resources in Higher Education*, Paris, United Nations Educational Scientific and Cultural Organisation and the International Association of Universities.

McMillan, S. (2002) 'Exploring models of interactivity from multiple research traditions: users, documents, and systems', in Livingstone, S. (ed.) *Handbook of New Media: Shaping and Consequences of ICTs*, London, Sage Publications.

Mann, S. (2001) 'Alternative perspectives on the student experience: alienation and engagement', *Studies in Higher Education*, 26 (1): 7–19.

Marton, F. and Booth, S. (1997) *Learning and Awareness*, New Jersey, Lawrence Erlbaum Associates.

Marton, F. and Säljö, R. (1976) 'On qualitative differences in learning I: outcome and process', *British Journal of Educational Technology*, 46: 4–11.

Metcalfe, J., Thomson, Q. and Green, H. (2002) *Improving Standards in Postgraduate Research Degree Programmes*, London, Joint Funding Councils Working Group.

Mezirow, J. (1990) *Fostering Critical Reflection in Adulthood*, San Francisco, Jossey-Bass Inc.

Middleton, S. (1997) *The Scholarship of Teaching*, http://www.uoguelph.ca/atguelph/98-02-27/sandy.html, accessed August 2004.

Miller, C. and Parlett, M. (1974) *Up to the Mark: A Study of the Examination Game*, London, The Society for Research into Higher Education.

Murray, H., Gillese, E., Lennon, M., Mercer, P. and Robinson, M. (1996) *Ethical Principles in University Teaching*, Vancouver, Society for Teaching and Learning in Higher Education.

Murray, R. (2003) *How to Survive your Viva*, Maidenhead, Open University Press.

National Committee of Inquiry into Higher Education (NCIHE) (1997a) *Higher Education in the Learning Society. Report of the National Inquiry into Higher Education* (The Dearing Report), London, HMSO.

National Committee of Inquiry into Higher Education (NCIHE) (1997b) *Report 6: Trends in Participation by Lower Socio-economic Group*, London, HMSO.

Naughton, J. (1999) *A Brief History of the Future*, London, Weidenfeld and Nicolson.

Nelson, B. (2002) *Striving for Quality, Teaching, Learning and Scholarship*, Canberra, Commonwealth of Australia.

Noble, K. (1994) *Changing Doctoral Degrees: An International Perspective*, Buckingham, The Society for Research in Higher Education and Open University Press.

Nonaka, I. (1994) 'A dynamic theory of organizational knowledge creation', *Organization Science*, 5 (1): 14–37.

Nuy, H. (1991) 'Interactions of study orientation and students' appreciations of structure in their educational environment', *Higher Education*, 22: 267–74.

Organisation for Economic Cooperation and Development (OECD) (2003) *Education at a Glance: OECD indicators 2003*, Paris, OECD.

Parry, S. (1998) 'Disciplinary discourses in doctoral theses', *Higher Education*, 36: 273–99.

Perkins, D. and Blythe, T. (1994) 'Putting understanding up front', *Educational Leadership*, 51 (5): 4–7.

Perry, W. (1970) *Forms of Intellectual and Ethical Development in the College Years*, New York, Holt Rhienhart Winston.

Phipps, R. and Merisotis, J. (1999) *What's the Difference?: A Review of Contemporary Research on the Effectiveness of Distance Learning in Higher Education*, http//www.ihep.com/Pubs/PDF/Difference.pdf, accessed July 2003.

Prosser, M. and Trigwell, K. (1999) *Understanding Learning and Teaching: The Experience of Higher Education*, Buckingham, The Society for Research in Higher Education and Open University Press.

The Quality Assurance Agency for Higher Education (QAA) (2001) *Subject Overview Report: Business and Management 2000 to 2001*, Gloucester, QAA.

Ramsden, P. (1987) 'Improving teaching and learning in higher education, the case for a relational perspective', *Studies in Higher Education* 12: 275–86.

Ramsden, P. (2003) *Learning to Teach in Higher Education*, Second Edition, RoutledgeFalmer, London.

Ramsden, P. and Entwistle, N. (1981) 'Effects of academic departments on student approaches to study', *British Journal of Educational Psychology*, 51: 367–83.

Reynolds, M. and Trehan, K. (2000) 'Assessment, a critical perspective', *Studies in Higher Education*, 25 (3): 267–78.

Riddell, S., Tinklin, T. and Wilson, A. (2002) 'Disabled students in higher education: the impact of anti-discrimination legislation on teaching, learning and assessment', paper presented at the ESRC seminar: Reconfiguring Sociology of Education, University of Bristol, 22 November (available from http://www.escalate.ac.uk/resources/disabledstudentsinhe/22Nova.rtf).

Roberts, G. (2003) *Set for Success: Review of Research Assessment*, London, Higher Education Funding Council, England.

Robins, K. and Webster, F. (2003) *The Virtual University: Knowledge, Markets and Management*, Oxford, Oxford University Press.

Rogers, C. (1969) *Freedom to Learn*, Columbus, Ohio, Charles E. Merrill.

Roschelle, J. and Teasley, S. (1995) 'The construction of shared knowledge in collaborative problem solving', in O'Malley, C. (ed.) *Computer Supported Collaborative Learning*, Berlin, Springer Verlag.

Ross, J. and Cousins, J. (1994). 'Brief research report: intentions to seek and give help, and behaviour in cooperative learning group', *Contemporary Educational Psychology*, 19: 476–82.

Rowland, S. (2000) *The Enquiring University Teacher*, Buckingham, The Society for Research in Higher Education and Open University Press.

Ryan, S., Scott, B., Freeman, H. and Patel, D. (2000) *The Virtual University: the Internet and Resource-Based Learning*, Open and Distance Learning Series, London, Kogan Page.

Salomon, D. and Perkins, D. (1998) 'Individual and social aspects of learning', *Review of Research in Education*, 23: 1–24.

Schön, D. (1983) *The Reflective Practitioner: How Professionals Think in Action*, New York, Basic Books.

Schön, D. (1987) *Educating the Reflective Practitioner*, San Francisco, Jossey-Bass.

Schrage, M. (1990) *Shared Minds*, New York, Random House.

Schramm, W. (1962) *Programmed Instruction: Today and Tomorrow*, New York, The Fund for the Advancement of Education.

Schwartz, S. (2004) 'Time to bid goodbye to the psychology lecture', *The Psychologist*, 17 (1), January.

Scott, P. (1995) *The Meanings of Mass Higher Education*, Buckingham, The Society for Research in Higher Education and Open University Press.

Scott, P. (ed.) (1998) *The Globalization of Higher Education*, Buckingham, The Society for Research in Higher Education and Open University Press.

Senge, P. (1993) *The Fifth Discipline: The Art and Practice of The Learning Organization*, London, Century Business.

Seufert, S. (2000) 'The net academy as a medium for learning communities', *Educational Technology and Society*, 3 (3): 122–36.

Shulman, L. (2000) 'From Minsk to Pinsk: why a scholarship of teaching and learning?' *Journal of Scholarship of Teaching and Learning (JoSoTL)*, 1: 48–52.

Silver, H. and and Silver, P. (1997) *Students: Changing Roles, Changing Lives*, Buckingham, The Society for Research in Higher Education and Open University Press.

Skinner, B. (1954) 'The science of learning and the art of teaching', *Harvard Educational Review*, 24 (1): 86–97.

Sklar, E. and Pollack, J. (2000) 'A framework for enabling an internet learning community', *Educational Technology and Society*, 3 (3): 393–408.

Snyder, B. (1971) *The Hidden Curriculum*, New York, Knopf.

Spector, J. (2000) 'Towards a philosophy of instruction', *Educational Technology and Society*, 3 (3): 522–5.

Staff and Educational Development Association (2002) *Staff and Educational Development Association*, http://www.seda.ac.uk/, accessed August 2004.

Stefani, L. (2003) 'What is staff and educational development?', in Khan, P. and Baume, D. (eds) *A Guide to Staff and Educational Development*, London, Kogan Page.

Stefani, L. and Elton, L. (2002) 'Continuing professional development of academic teachers through self initiated learning', *Assessment and Evaluation in Higher Education*, 27 (2): 117–30.

Stefani, L. and Matthew, R. (2002) 'The difficulties of defining development: a case study', *International Journal of Academic Development*, 7 (1): 41–50.

Stefani, L. and Nicol, D. (1997) 'From teacher to facilitator of collaborative enquiry', in Armstrong, S., Brown, S. and Thompson G. (eds) *Facing up to Radical Changes in Universities and Colleges*, London: Kogan Page.

Stenmark, D. (2002) 'Group cohesiveness and extrinsic motivation in virtual groups, lessons from an action case study of electronic brainstorming', in *Proceedings of the 35th Hawaii International Conference on System Sciences*, Washington, IEEE Computer Society.

Sturt, R. (1981) 'Disability', in Warren Piper, D. (ed.) *Is Higher Education Fair?*, Guildford, The Society for Research into Higher Education.

Tansley, C. and Bryson, C. (2000) 'Virtual seminars, a viable substitute for traditional approaches?' *Innovations in Education and Training International*, 37 (4): 335–45.

Themessl-Hubber, M. and Grutsch, M. (2003) 'The shifting locus of control in participatory evaluations', *Evaluation*, 9 (1): 92–111.

Thompson, L. (1997) *Professional Development for Online Learning*, http://www.nw97. edu.au/public/papers/thompson.html, accessed April 2004.

Tight, M. (2003) *Researching Higher Education*, Buckingham, The Society for Research in Higher Education and Open University Press.

Tinkler, P. and Jackson, C. (2000) 'Examining the doctorate, institutional policy and the PhD examination process in Britain', *Studies in Higher Education*, 25 (2): 167–80.

Trigwell, K. (1995) 'Increasing faculty understanding of teaching', in Wright, W. (ed.) *Teaching Improvement Practices: Successful Strategies for Higher Education*, Bolton, MA, Anker.

Trigwell, K., Martin, E., Benjamin, J. and Prosser, M. (2000) 'Scholarship of teaching: a model', *Higher Education Research and Development*, 19 (2): 3–5.

Trow, M. (1973) *Problems in the Transition from Elite to Mass Higher Education*, Berkely, CA, Carnegie Commission on Higher Education.

Trowler, P. (1998) *Academics Responding to Change: New Higher Education Frameworks and Academic Cultures*, Buckingham, The Society for Research in Higher Education and Open University Press.

Trowler, P (2003) *Education Policy*, Second Edition, London, Routledge.

UK Council for Graduate Education (UKCGE) (1995) *Graduate Schools*, Lichfield, Staffs, UKCGE.

UK Grad Programme (2004) *Proceedings from the UK GRAD Policy Forum: The implementation of the Roberts' recommendations on training requirements*, Manchester, 7–8 January 2004, http://www.grad.ac.uk/downloads/forum/robertsforum_report.pdf, accessed April 2005

Universities Grant Committee (UGC) (1964) *Report of the Committee on University Teaching Methods* (The Hale Report), London, HMSO.

Universities Grant Committee (UGC) (1975) *Statistics of Education: Volume 6 Universities*, London, HMSO.

Usher, R. (2002) 'A diversity of doctorates, fitness for the knowledge economy?', *Higher Education Research and Development*, 21 (2): 143–53.

Van Dijk, J. (1999) *The Network Society: Social Aspects of New Media*, London, Sage.

Van Manen, M. (1991) 'Reflectivity and the pedagogical moment: the normativity of pedagogical thinking and acting', *Journal of Curriculum Studies*, 23: 507–36.

Veen, W., Lam, I. and Taconis, R. (1998) 'A virtual workshop as a tool for collaboration: towards a model of telematics learning environments', *Computers and Education* 30 (1–2): 31–9.

Vermunt, J. (1998) 'The regulation of constructive learning processes', *British Journal of Educational Psychology*, 68: 149–71.

Watson, D. and Bowden, R. (2002) *The New University Decade 1992–2002*, Brighton, Educational Research Centre, University of Brighton.

Webb, G. (1996) *Understanding Staff Development*, Buckingham, The Society for Research into Higher Education and Open University Press.

Wegerif, R. (1998) 'The social dimension of asynchronous learning networks', *Journal of Asynchronous Learning Networks*, 2: 34–49.

Weil, S. (1997) 'Postgraduate education and lifelong learning as collaborative inquiry in action, an emergent model', in Burgess, R. (ed.) *Beyond the First Degree: Graduate Education, Lifelong Learning and Careers*, Buckingham, The Society for Research into Higher Education and Open University Press.

Weimer, M. (1997) 'Assumptions that devalue university teaching' *International Journal for Academic Development*, 2 (1): 52–60.

Wenger, E. (1999) *Communities of Practice: Learning, Meaning, and Identity*, Cambridge, Cambridge University Press.

Wertsch, J. (1991) 'A sociocultural approach to socially shared cognition', in Resnick, L.,

Levine, J. and Teasley, S. (eds) *Perspectives on Socially Shared Cognition*, Arlington VA, American Psychological Association.

Wiersema, N. (2000) *How Does Collaborative Learning Actually Work in a Classroom and how do Students React to it?: A Brief Recollection*, http://www.lgu.ac.uk/deliberations/collab.learning/wiersema.html, accessed January 2004.

Williams, S. (1977) *Robbins Plus Twenty: Which Way for Higher Education?*, London, Birkbeck College.

Winfield, G. (1987) *The Social Science PhD: The ESRC Inquiry on Submission Rates*, London, Economic and Social Research Council.

Winter, R., Griffiths, M. and Green, K. (1997) 'The "academic" qualities of practice, what are the criteria for a practice based PhD?', *Studies in Higher Education*, 25: 25–37.

Woodley, A. (1981) 'Age Bias', in Warren Piper, D. (ed.) *Is Higher Education Fair?*, Guildford, The Society for Research into Higher Education.

Woolf, A. (2002) *Does Education Matter?: Myths about Education and Economic Growth*, London, Penguin Books.

Zenios, M. and Steeples, C. (2003) 'Developing and delivering pedagogically informed technology for meaningful learning experiences within institutions, action points for creating e-learning centres', in Banks, S., Goodyear, P., Hodgson, V., Jones, C., Lally, V., McConnell, D. and Steeples, C. (2004) *Networked Learning 2004: A Research Based Conference on E-Learning in Higher Education and Lifelong Learning*, Lancaster University and Sheffield University.

Zuber-Skerritt, O. (1992) *Professional Development in Higher Education*, London, Kogan Page.

Zuber-Skerritt, O. and Ryan, Y. (1994) *Quality in Postgraduate Education*, London, Kogan Page.

Index